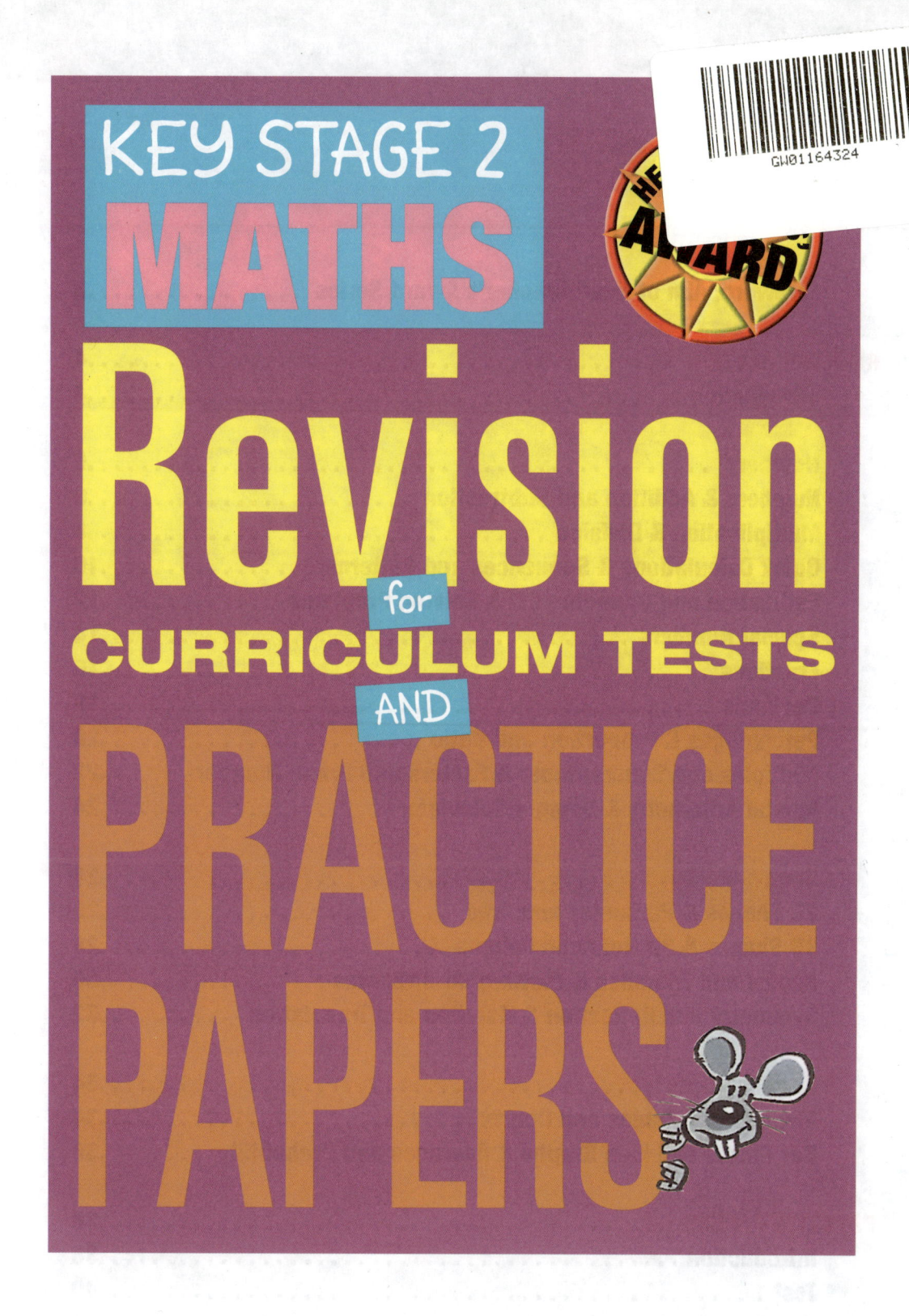

KEY STAGE 2
MATHS
Revision
for CURRICULUM TESTS AND
PRACTICE PAPERS

Author
Camilla de la Bédoyère

Consultant Editor
John Cattermole

This is a Flame Tree Book
First published in 2002

07 08 09 10 11

10 9 8 7 6 5 4 3

ISBN 1-903817-70-6

Flame Tree is part of
The Foundry Creative Media Company Ltd
Crabtree Hall, Crabtree Lane, Fulham,
London SW6 6TY

Visit our website: www.flametreepublishing.com

Copyright © The Foundry 2007

Thanks to Dave Jones for the technical illustrations.

Thanks also to Vicky Garrard, Julia Rolf, Colin Rudderham, Graham Stride, Nick Wells and Polly Willis.

All rights reserved. No part of this publication may be reproduced, stored in a retrieval system, or transmitted in any form or by any means, electronic, mechanical, photocopying, recording or otherwise, without the prior permission of the publisher.

A copy of the CIP data for this book is available from the British Library

Printed in China

Contents

Foreword: Aim of Head Teacher's Award Series 3

REVISION SECTION 4
Introduction 4

Numbers 6
Numbers & Addition and Subtraction 6
Multiplication & Division 8
Quick Calculations & Sequences and Patterns 10
Estimation and Rounding Off & Solving Problems 12
Special Numbers 14
Fractions 16
Decimals 18
Percentages & Proportion and Ratio 20
Multiples and Square Roots & Factors and Prime Numbers 22
Mental Arithmetic & Using a Calculator .24

Shape and Space 26
2D Shapes & Perimeter and Area 26
3D Shapes & 3D Nets and Volume 28
Angles and Triangles & Plotting Co-ordinates 30
Symmetry and Reflection & Rotation and Translation 32

Handling Data 34
Measuring & Tables and Charts 34
Bar Charts and Line Graphs & Averages and Probability 36

PRACTICE PAPERS 38
Introduction 38
Test 1 40
Test 2 54
Test 3: Mental Arithmetic Instructions and Questions 68
Test 4: Level 6 69
Glossary 74
Answers: Tests 1, 2 & 4 75
Answers: Mental Arithmetic Test & Revision Section Questions . . .78
Test 3: Mental Arithmetic Answer Sheet 79

Foreword

In today's ever-changing educational climate in which targets, levels of achievement and school league-tables grab headline news, it is important to remember what is at the core of it all: the education of your child.

Children learn at different speeds and achieve different levels during their early years at school, so it is important that a child is encouraged to work to the best of his or her ability, whatever their standard.

The Head Teacher Awards, which many schools use, is a simple, yet highly effective way to motivate children. In the classroom a child may be given an HTA for a particularly good piece of work, or for trying hard in a subject they struggle with, or for neat handwriting, fluent reading, or imaginative creative writing. The list is endless, yet the effect of the HTA on the child is great: they feel valued and that something they have really tried hard at has been noticed.

The idea behind the Head Teacher's Award Series is much the same as the award-scheme practised in the classroom. This book has been devised for use by children who are coming up to their National Tests at the end of Key Stage Two. Not only does it reinforce all the information they need to know for their Tests through a series of fun and practical questions and activities, it gives children a chance to work a little harder and be rewarded with a Head Teacher's Award. Throughout the book, one or two questions on each page have a HTA symbol next to them, indicating that that particular question or activity may require a little more work or a more lateral approach in order to get the answer right. It is up to the parent to decide what the award should be (we are not advocating bribery here!), something to make the child feel they have reached a target. It may be that you decide with your child that they have to get a certain number of HTAs in the book before they can have their 'award', based on their ability.

Written by an author with great experience of Key Stage Two children, the aim of this book is that through a combination of revision, motivational aids and practical tests that the child can take in a familiar and comfortable environment, they will be as prepared as they can be for the National Tests that they will take at the end of Key Stage Two.

John Foster
Former Head Teacher of St Marks Junior School, Salisbury.

Introduction

What are SATs?

Children who are in Years 3 to 6 study Key Stage 2 of the National Curriculum. At the end of Year 6, in May, the children are tested on their knowledge and skills in three core subjects: Mathematics, English and Science. The tests are commonly known as SATs, which stands for Standard Assessment Tasks, or NCTs (National Curriculum Tests). The teachers use the SATs results, as well as continuous assessment that is conducted in the classroom, to assess how well the children are doing.

How this Book Works

By the time your child takes their SATs they should have covered everything in the National Curriculum that they are meant to know. This book is not intended to teach new subjects in mathematics, but should be used as an aid to revision and improving exam technique.

Revision Section
The essentials of the mathematics curriculum are covered with clear explanations and examples. On the pages you will find key words or concepts highlighted to help your child remember them.

Parent's Guides
These feature regularly throughout the book and may:
- Explain why a topic is important.
- Suggest what you can do to reinforce your child's learning of a topic.
- Give examples of activities you can do together.

Questions
Quick questions feature throughout the book. By answering the questions your child will reinforce the concepts they have just covered in the text. Answering the questions correctly gives the children confidence and motivates them to continue working their way through the book.

Head Teacher's Award
Throughout the book Head Teacher's Award questions (HTAs) feature. These are slightly harder than the other questions. Achieving a high standard in answering Head Teacher's Award questions earns your child the HTA.

Practice Papers
This is the section where your child can practise using the skills they have revised. There are four practice papers, including a Level 6 extension. These are explained in more detail on page 38. Answers and a marking scheme are included.

What You Can Do to Help

Encourage your child to complete the questions and activities that are included in the revision section. Practice really consolidates learning and will be greatly beneficial to your child. Answering questions together will also help you identify any particular difficulties your child is having.

Promote good learning habits. Encourage your child to plan their revision, allowing plenty of time for breaks. They will learn and retain more in two periods of 20 minutes with a five-minute break than an unbroken 45-minute period. Teach them to revisit a topic regularly, so that it becomes part of their long-term memory.

Motivate your child to succeed. Reward your child for every HTA they get – discuss this with your child and agree a suitable reward.

A healthy body keeps a mind active. Ensure that your child eats a well-balanced and healthy diet, gets plenty of exercise and a full night's sleep every night.

Keep the tests in perspective. Remember that SATs are as much a test of the school's success as of your child's ability, so do not cause your child anxiety by over-stressing the importance of the exams. Nor are SATs an end in themselves: they are part of a whole process designed to ensure that your child has a solid foundation for later learning and success.

Numbers

Pick a Number!

Numbers are the basic tools of mathematics – you can't bake a cake without ingredients and you can't do sums without numbers.

Digits

All numbers are made up of digits:
1 2 3 4 5 6 7 8 9 0.

A three-digit number looks like this: 875
This number is eight hundred and seventy-five.

A five-digit number looks like this: 25 439
This number is twenty-five thousand, four-hundred and thirty-nine.

Questions
1) Write down these numbers in words: 8297, 10 004, 514, 999.
2) How many digits are there in
a) one million b) one thousand c) ten?
3) Look at the digits underlined in these numbers. What is the value of each of them?
a) 2 3_7_1
b) _99_ 961

Activity
Remember! Noughts may look like nothing but they do matter! Write down some big numbers with noughts in the middle. If you take the noughts out, what happens to the numbers?

The value of a digit depends on its **place** in the number line: the digits to the left are greater in value than the ones on the right.

millions	hundred-thousands	ten-thousands	thousands	hundreds	tens	units
2	7	6	2	9	8	4

This number is two million, seven hundred and sixty-two thousand, nine hundred and eighty-four and it looks like this: **2 762 984**.

Parent's Guide
Write down some large numbers together. Talk about which digits represent thousands, hundreds, tens and units. Can your child read the numbers out to you correctly? See if they can now place the numbers in order of size, starting with the smallest.

Numbers

Addition and Subtraction

Addition

Addition means adding up. Other words, such as **total**, **sum** and **increase** are sometimes used to mean **add**.

EXAMPLE:
Step One: Write out the numbers in columns and add the units first.

hundreds   tens   units
```
   H    T    U
   6    2    6
+  3    5    1
   ─────────────
```

Remember
If you don't put the numbers in the correct column you'll get the answer **wrong**.

Step Two: Add the units column first, then the tens, then the hundreds.

```
   H    T    U
   2    7    5
+  3    5    1
   ─────────────
   6    2    6
        1
```

You need to carry over the 1 from the tens to the hundreds.
What do you notice about these two calculations?

Subtraction

Subtraction, or taking away, is just the **opposite of adding**.

EXAMPLE:
Put the numbers in columns but be sure to **put the biggest number at the top** and **line up the units**. Always start with the units and borrow from the next column, if you need to.

```
     H    T    U
    ⁵6   ¹2    6
  −  3    5    1
     ─────────────
     2    7    5
```

Questions
1. Gus the Gorilla has 12 fewer oranges than Billy the Baboon, who has 36. How many oranges does Gus have?
2. Increase 356 by 789.
3. Peter collected 5329 stamps for the school charity. Samantha collected 8123. What was the difference between the numbers?
4. Using the hundreds, tens and units method, work out the following:
a) 543 − 319
b) 1000 − 956
c) 271 − 199

Activities
1. Starting with 723 add on in 3s and see how far you can go e.g. 723, 726, 729....
2. Now start with 1828 and count backwards, taking away 10 each time e.g. 1828, 1818, 1808 ... bet you can't get down to zero!

HEADTEACHER'S AWARD

Numbers

Multiplication

Multiplying is the same as *times*. You *have* to know your times tables to be able to multiply properly, so if you don't know them yet – get practising!

There are different ways to work out a multiplication on paper and it doesn't matter which method you use, as long as you are comfortable with it.

Remember
Always show your working out clearly and you could earn extra points, even if you get the answer wrong.

```
   25
 x 32
 ----
   50
  750
 ----
  800
```

x	20	5	+
30	600	150	750
2	40	10	50
			800

Simple Solutions
Some multiplications are easier than they look.

EXAMPLE:
If you had to multiply 75 by 9 you could multiply it by 10 first, then take 75 away:

$$75 \times 10 = 750$$
$$750 - 75 = 675$$

so $75 \times 9 = 675$

Simple!

Questions
1. $54 \times 6 = \ldots\ldots$
2. $236 \times 12 = \ldots\ldots$

Activity
Fizzbuzz

Take it in turns to count aloud. Numbers in the 5 times table should be replaced by 'fizz' and numbers in the 7 times table by 'buzz'. Thirty-five should be replaced by 'fizzbuzz'. Do you know why? What is the next 'fizzbuzz'?

Parent's Guide
Your child has probably learnt several different ways of multiplying and dividing but they will all depend on a sound knowledge of the times tables. If your child has a sound knowledge of times tables up to 10, challenge them to learn their tables up to 20.

Numbers

Division

Division means sharing. Sometimes you might say a small number goes into a bigger number. Dividing is the opposite of multiplying.

EXAMPLE:

75 divided by 3 is 25, or 3 into 75 goes 25 times.

There are two ways of doing division on paper: short division and long division. You have probably learnt both of them, but you can choose whichever method you prefer.

EXAMPLE:

short division

$$7 \overline{)8\ ^12\ ^54}\quad \begin{array}{c}1\ \ 1\ \ 7\end{array}\ r\ 5$$

long division

```
        1  1  7   r 5
    7 / 8  2  4
        7
        ‾‾
        1 2
          7
          ‾‾
          5 4
          4 9
          ‾‾
            5
```

Questions

Orwell the pig is King of the Farmyard. He decides to share out the cabbages between all the animals. There are 89 cabbages and 6 animals, including him.

1. How many cabbages do they get each?
2. How many cabbages are left over?
3. Half the animals have four legs, half have two legs. How many legs are there altogether?

Activity

Can you make up a problem like the one above? Make sure that multiplication and divisions have to be done to complete the whole question.

Tip

Have a guess at what the answer might be before you begin – it will help you imagine the numbers as real things, not just squiggles on the page.

Remember

The remainder (r) is the bit left over that you can't share out any further.

Numbers

Quick Calculations

Times 10

You can multiply by a 10, 100 or 1000 by adding on zeros:

18 x 10 = 180
18 x 100 = 1800
18 x 1000 = 18 000

You can divide by doing the opposite:

75 000 ÷ 10 = 7500
75 000 ÷ 100 = 750
75 000 ÷1000 = 75

Times 20

If you have to multiply by 20 you could double the number first, then add a zero:

27 x 20 = ?

27 x 2 = 54
then add a zero
= 540

Pots of Money

Multiplying or dividing money sums are just like other sums – but you must remember to put a decimal point and pound sign in the answer.

EXAMPLE:

£ 5.61
x   3
£ 16.83

£ 91.22
2)£182.44

Questions

1. 45 x 200 = ...
2. £29.03 x 4 = ...

Activity

To multiply 62 by 11 just add the two digits together (6 + 2 = 8) and put the total in the middle of the number to get the answer (682). Clever, huh? Try multiplying some other two-digit numbers by 11 using this method.

Parent's Guide

Children are expected to be able to do calculations in their heads and they learn many techniques at school to help them. Number patterns and sequences help them to do this. Write out the 9 times table with your child. Can you see an obvious pattern in the answers? What do the digits add up to?

Numbers

Sequences and Patterns

Number Sequences

A number sequence is a special list of numbers. If you look at them closely you will be able to work out what number comes next:

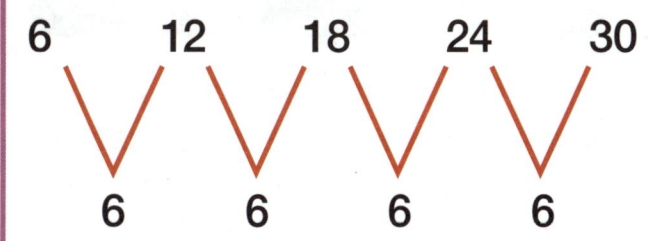

6   12   18   24   30
 \ / \ / \ / \ /
  6   6   6   6

The answer is 36 because the **difference** between each number is 6.

Sometimes the difference between the numbers also changes, following a pattern:

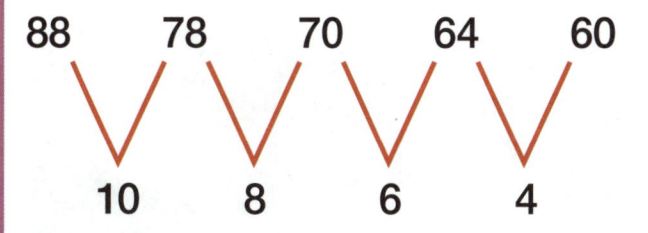

88   78   70   64   60
 \ / \ / \ / \ /
  10   8   6   4

What number comes next?
The answer is 58 because the **difference** each time decreases by 2.

Picture Patterns

You might get a question that has pictures instead of numbers. The question could ask 'How many mice will there be in the 8th picture?'.

Questions
Can you predict the next number?
1. 4, 8, 16, 32, 64, ?
2. 1, 4, 9, 16, 25, ?
What is the 12th number in this sequence?
14, 21, 28, 35, 42, . . .

Activity
Make up your own number sequences and see if someone else can spot the patterns. Use pictures to illustrate the sequences.

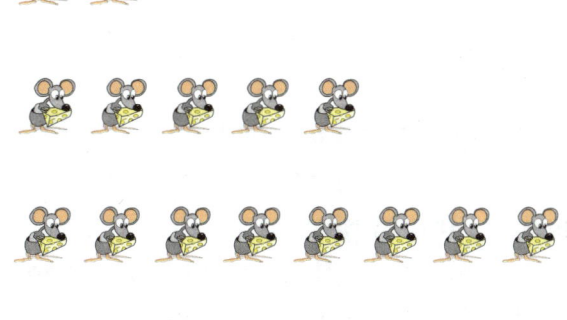

Work it out like this:

- 3 mice are added each time.
- By the 8th picture there will be **7 lots of 3** mice added to the first picture.
- So we have to do this sum: 7 × 3 = 21.
- Then add on the two mice from the first picture: 21 + 2 = 23.
- The answer is: there will be 23 mice in the 8th picture.

Numbers

Estimation & Rounding Off

Estimation

Estimating means *making a good guess*. It can be very helpful when you are doing calculations because it helps you check you've got the right answer, once you have done the sum.

EXAMPLE:

Michael is told to work out how many cars are needed to transport 37 cubs to camp. He knows 3 cubs will fit in each car and he knows that 3 goes into 37 about 12 times (an estimate). He works out that 12 x 3 = 36. This leaves 1 cub without a ride – so he tells his cub leader that 13 cars will be needed for the journey.

Activity

Try some estimates of your own. Look at a tin of beans. How much does it weigh? Now think about yourself. Can you estimate how much you weigh? How much does another person in your family weigh? Estimate first!

Rounding Off

Rounding off is another way of getting close to the right answer. It is useful because it can give us an *approximate answer* more easily than doing a long calculation. We normally round off to the nearest 10, 100 or 1000.

EXAMPLE:

1055 rounded to the nearest
- 10 is 1060
- 100 is 1100
- 1000 is 1000

Remember
Round off to the nearest number, either up or down. If the number is in the middle of two possible answers round it up.

Questions
1. Round off these numbers to the nearest ten:
15, 74, 99, 116
2. Round off these numbers to the nearest hundred:
678, 1802, 555

Parent's Guide

Children are required to estimate answers to their calculations and use this information to check their results. This encourages them to think about the context of the problem they are working on. Look at Michael's problem with the cars. Ask your child what would have happened to the final cub if Michael had relied on his estimate.

Get your child to estimate and then measure the length of things in the house: this book, a table, a door, their bed.

12

Numbers

Solving Real Problems

Problems with Money

Some questions ask you to work out what is **best value for money**.

Asif can get a book of 6 bus tickets for £1.50 or buy them individually for 30p each. He works out that the bus tickets cost only 25p each if he buys the book (150p ÷ 6 = 25p). This is **better value** than buying them one at a time.

Weighing it Up

A jar of peanut butter costs £2.25 for 150 g and a jar of chocolate spread costs £1.75 for 100 g. Which is better value?

You can work out problems like these by calculating the **price per unit**.

In other words, how much does one gram of each cost?

For each one, work out: PRICE ÷ WEIGHT

Peanut butter: 225p ÷ 150 g = 1.5p per gram
Chocolate spread: 175p ÷ 100 g = 1.75p per gram

So the peanut butter, being cheaper, is better value.

Tip
Use a calculator to help with these questions.

Remember
Price per unit = price ÷ weight

Questions
1. If you buy two packets of biscuits for 57p you get the third one free. How much does each one cost?
2. Round off your answer to the nearest 10.
3. How many packets of biscuits would you get for £2.28?

Activity
When you go to the supermarket look at the prices of products that are on 'special offer'. Can you use a calculator to work out how much money you would really save? Sometimes 'special offers' are not really that special after all!

13

Numbers

Special Numbers 1

Some numbers are given special names – you will need to learn these carefully.

Even Numbers

Even numbers can all be divided by 2, without a remainder.

2, 4, 6, 8, 10, 12, 14 …

Tip
Did you know that if you add two even numbers together, you always get an even number?

Odd Numbers

Odd numbers all give a remainder when divided by 2.

1, 3, 5, 7, 9, 11, 13 …

What happens when you add any two odd numbers together?

Now add an even and an odd number together. Is the answer odd or even?

Square Numbers

When a number is multiplied by *itself* the answer is a square number.

$2 \times 2 = 4 = 2^2$

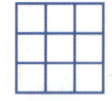

$3 \times 3 = 9 = 3^2$

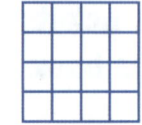

$4 \times 4 = 16 = 4^2$

Cube Numbers

When a number is multiplied by *itself three times* the answer is a cube number.

$1 \times 1 \times 1 = 1 = 1^3$

$2 \times 2 \times 2 = 8 = 2^3$

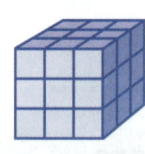

$3 \times 3 \times 3 = 27 = 3^3$

Questions
1. Work out the first 10 square numbers.
2. Work out the first 6 cube numbers.

Activity
Can you work out why these numbers are called 'square' and 'cube' numbers? Look at the pictures for a big clue!

Parent's Guide
Square numbers can be used to calculate area and cube numbers can be used to calculate volume – subjects that will be covered later in this book. Negative numbers can cause problems for some children. Encourage the use of a number line to help your child gain confidence.

Numbers

Number Lines

Negative Numbers

Number lines help us to understand negative numbers. We can place whole numbers, integers, on a number line to see how they all fit together. A number line can go on forever, in either direction!

-5 -4 -3 -2 -1 0 +1 +2 +3 +4 +5

Adding and Subtracting Negative Numbers

When you have to add or subtract negative numbers, draw a number line and count along.

Count to the right to add, count to the left to subtract.

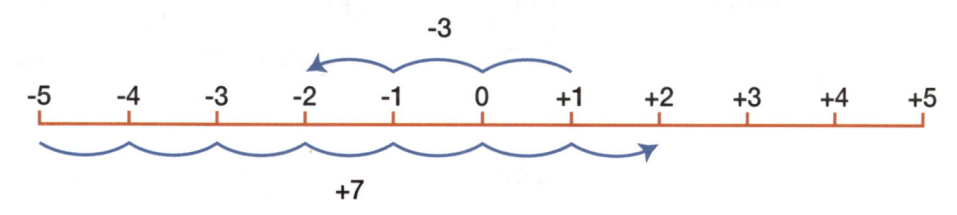

-3
-5 -4 -3 -2 -1 0 +1 +2 +3 +4 +5
+7

EXAMPLE: $1 - 3 = -2$ $-5 + 7 = 2$

Remember
Negative numbers are less than zero. We use them when we talk about temperature or money. If you have -£50 in the bank it means you owe the bank £50. Bad luck!

Some Useful Symbols
> This symbol means 'more than'
    10 > -10   True or false?
    -2 > -5   True or false?
< This symbol means 'less than'
    -1 < 0   True or false?
    -2 < -12   True or false?

Questions
1. Put these numbers in order, using the symbols for 'more than' and 'less than'. Start with the lowest number.
45   -10   -1   16   208   -311   0   2
2. -8 + 12 = ...
3. What is an integer?

Activity
Look in the newspaper to discover temperatures around the world. You will see that in some countries the temperature goes below zero. The higher the negative number, the colder it is.

HEADTEACHER'S AWARD

Numbers

Fractions

Fractions tell us how something has been divided up. A cake that has been cut up into pieces has been **divided into fractions**.

A fraction has two parts:

$\frac{3}{4}$ the top part is the **numerator**
the bottom part is the **denominator**

Remember
The denominator tells us how many pieces the whole has been cut up into. The numerator tells us how many pieces we are talking about.

Would you rather have $\frac{1}{4}$ of this cake, or $\frac{3}{4}$ of it?

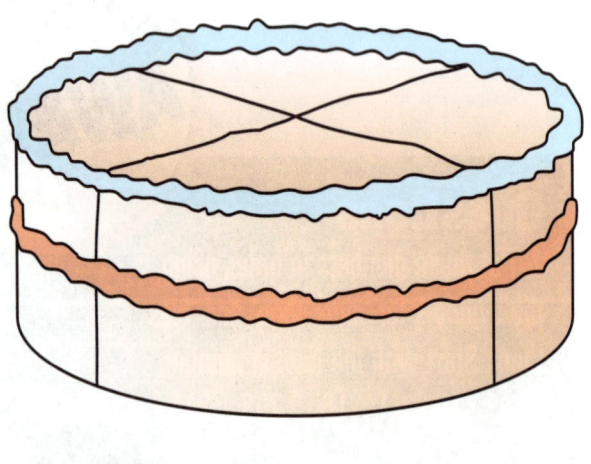

Questions
Use the number line shown to do the following sums:
1. $-1 + 2\frac{1}{2} = $ ……
2. $0 - 1\frac{1}{2} = $ ……

Activity
Look at your ruler. It is divided into centimetres and millimetres. Each millimetre is a fraction of a centimetre: it is one tenth, or $\frac{1}{10}$. How many tenths are there in half a centimetre? Can you write this as a fraction?

Fractions and Number Lines

Here is another number line. There are whole numbers (integers) on it, but this time some fractions (halves) have been marked on too. Can you see where the quarters would be?

-2　$\frac{1}{2}$　-1　$\frac{1}{2}$　0　$\frac{1}{2}$　1　$\frac{1}{2}$　2　$\frac{1}{2}$　3

Parent's Guide
Use squared paper to show your child how different fractions can mean the same thing (equivalent fractions). For example, $\frac{1}{4} = \frac{2}{8}$ and $\frac{2}{10} = \frac{1}{5}$. Talk about the names we give fractions (one quarter, three fifths, etc.) and make sure they are comfortable with the vocabulary.

16

Numbers

Fun with Fractions

Fraction Bars

Drawing fractions can make them easier to understand. These diagrams are called **fraction bars** and they are useful when we need to see how **big** a fraction is. They can also show us when fractions are **equivalent** – when two fractions mean the same thing.

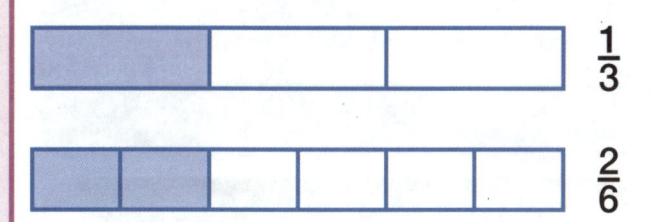

$\frac{1}{3}$

$\frac{2}{6}$

You can see that $\frac{1}{3}$ is the same, or equivalent, to $\frac{2}{6}$.

Questions

Use a fraction bar to change these fractions so they both have a denominator of 8.
1. $\frac{1}{2}$
2. $\frac{1}{4}$
3. Can you now add them to $\frac{1}{8}$ and make a new fraction?

Activity

Find 20 pennies and see if you can divide them into quarters, halves and tenths. How many pennies do you have in one quarter? How many do you have in a half? How many do you have in a tenth? Does this remind you of your times tables?

Tip

Make sure your fraction bars are the same size.

Comparing Fractions

You have three fractions:

$\frac{1}{2}$ $\frac{3}{4}$ $\frac{5}{12}$

You can use fraction bars to work out which fraction is bigger:

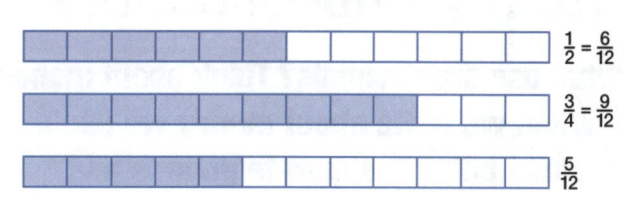

$\frac{1}{2} = \frac{6}{12}$

$\frac{3}{4} = \frac{9}{12}$

$\frac{5}{12}$

You can see that:

$\frac{9}{12} > \frac{6}{12} > \frac{5}{12}$

so:

$\frac{3}{4} > \frac{1}{2} > \frac{5}{12}$

17

Numbers

Decimals 1

Back at the beginning of the book we talked about digits. We said that the digits on the left of a number are bigger than those on the right. When we use decimals we have some more digits. They are placed on the right of the units, with a decimal point to separate them.

tens → units ← tenths
195.46
hundreds → ← hundredths

Decimals, like fractions, are useful for talking about 'between whole numbers'. The number above can be described as more than 195, but less than 196.

Money and Decimals

What use are decimals? Think about money – when we write about money we use a decimal point to separate pounds and pence. A pound is divided into hundredths but we call them 'pence' or 'pennies'.

Decimals on Number Lines

Look at decimals on a number line.

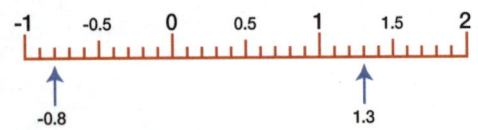

-1   -0.5   0   0.5   1   1.5   2
         ↑   ↑
       -0.8   1.3

Each whole number is divided into **tenths**. They could be divided further into hundreds, thousandths or even millionths – they could go on forever.

You can use the number line to work out the size of decimal numbers and put them in order.

Remember
You can round off decimals the same way you round off integers.

Questions
1. Put these numbers in order of size, starting with the smallest:
9.76   0.01   7.02   2.4   -1.9   7.2
2. Round off these numbers to the nearest whole number:
0.78   2.49   1.91   103.5

Activity
Americans call their pennies 'cents'. Can you find out what 'cent' means in French? Think of as many words as you can that start with 'cent…'?

Parent's Guide
Once children understand decimals they can get to grips with metric measurements. Use a tape measure, measuring jugs and weighing scales to show your child how we measure using decimals. See if they can convert centimetres to metres and round off to the nearest tenth.

Decimals 2

Changing Fractions into Decimals

Look at this fraction bar:
You can see that it represents $\frac{5}{10}$ or $\frac{1}{2}$.

Can you convert $\frac{5}{10}$ to a decimal

number? It looks like this:

units   tenths
     0.5

0 = units and 5 = tenths, so you have written $\frac{5}{10}$ or five tenths.

Sometimes converting fractions to decimals is not so easy and you may want to use a **calculator** to help you.

Tip
To convert decimals using a calculator divide the numerator by the denominator.

EXAMPLE:
$\frac{5}{8} = 3 \div 8 = 0.375$

Adding and Subtracting Decimals

You can add or subtract decimals just as you do with normal numbers. It is important that the decimal points are in line when doing so:

```
  5.25        6.94
 +3.04       -2.71
 -----       -----
  8.29        4.23
```

Multiplying and Dividing Decimals

When you **multiply** a decimal number by 10, you just move the digits **one** place to the **left**.

EXAMPLE:
34.56 x 10 = 345.6

Look at it this way:
34.56 x 10 =

H	T	U	.	tenths	hundredths
	3	4	.	5	6
3	4	5	.	6	

Tip
To multiply by 100 simply move the digit **two** places to the **left**.

EXAMPLE:
0.76 x 100 = 76

0.76 x 100

H	T	U	.	tenths	hundredths
		0	.	7	6
	7	6	.	0	

Can you see how the value of each digit increases?

Questions

Complete questions 1. and 2. with paper and pencil. Use a calculator for question 3.
1. 7.86 + 0.52 = ...
2. 145.09 − 23.04 = ...
3. Turn these fractions into decimals: $\frac{5}{8}, \frac{3}{4}, \frac{3}{20}$.

Activity

Work out how you **divide** decimal numbers by 10 and 100. Here's a clue — it is just like multiplying decimals, but the opposite!

Numbers

Percentages

Per cent means 'out of 100'. We use percentages, like fractions and decimals, to talk about parts of a whole. The sign for per cent is %.

Remember
50% means 50 out of a hundred, which is the same as saying $\frac{50}{100}$ or $\frac{5}{10}$ or $\frac{1}{2}$ or 0.5.

EXAMPLE:
Look at the percentages on this fraction bar:

$\frac{1}{4}$

40%

Imagine they are bars of chocolate. Would you rather have 40% of one, or $\frac{1}{4}$ of the other?

Converting Percentages

- To convert percentages to decimals **divide by 100** by moving the digits two places to the right.

EXAMPLE:
18% = 18 ÷ 100 or $\frac{18}{100}$ = 18.0
= 0.18

- To convert decimals to percentages **multiply by 100** by moving the digits two places to the left.

EXAMPLE:
0.03 = 0.03 x 100 = 0.03
= 3%

- To convert percentages to fractions is even easier because a percentage is **out of 100**.

EXAMPLE:
35% = $\frac{35}{100}$

Short Cuts
To work out 10% of something divide by 10:
10% of 75 = 7.5

To work out 20% divide by 10 then double your answer:
10% of 15 = 7.5
so 20% of 75 = 15

Questions
1. What is 10% of 260?
2. What is 20% of 260?
3. What is 5% of 260?

Activity
See if you can make your own short cuts for calculating 60%, 25%, 75%. Test your short cuts to make sure they work.

Parent's Guide
Point out to your child the situations in real life where percentages are used to pass on information – newspapers, television and shops. Encourage them to estimate percentages for themselves, e.g. 'What percentage of cars, do you think, are white?'

Numbers

Proportion and Ratio

Proportion

We know that percentages mean 'out of a hundred' or 'parts of a hundred', but do we always have to talk about part of a whole as part of a hundred?

Look at this egg box. There are 5 eggs still there – we could say that 5 out of 6 eggs are left. We are then describing the proportion of eggs that are left in the box.

We can write it like this:

The proportion of eggs that is left is 5:6

What proportion of eggs has been eaten?

Ratio

A ratio is a comparison between two numbers.

Derek the builder has to make some render to repair a brick wall. He mixes the ingredients – sand and cement – to make the render.

Derek always mixes one lot of cement to three lots of sand.

It doesn't matter how much render Derek needs, he always has to mix his ingredients in the same ratio.

We write it like this:

The ratio of cement to sand is 1:3

What is the ratio of sand to cement?

Questions
1. Draw 10 small circles and shade in 3 of them. What proportion is now unshaded?
2. What proportion is shaded?
3. What is the ratio of shaded circles to unshaded circles?

Activity
Ask a grown-up to help you make some fairy cakes. Try to double up the recipe; you will need to keep the ratio of eggs to fat and flour the same, or the cakes won't rise. If you are successful you'll have lots of cakes. Worth the effort!

Numbers

Multiples/Square Roots

Multiples

Look at these number sequences:

2   4   6   8   10   12   14

7   14   21   28   35   42

Do you recognise the patterns? The first sequence contains numbers from the 2 times table. These numbers are called multiples of 2. The second sequence contains some multiples of 7.

Tip
Multiples of 10 all end in 0.
Multiples of 5 end in 5 or 0.
Multiples of 2 end in 0, 2, 4, 6 or 8.

Square Roots

On page 14 we learnt that when a number is multiplied by itself the answer is a square number:

8 x 8 = 64 = 8²

We call the number that is multiplied by itself the **square root**.

9 x 9 = 81
9 is the square root of 81.
We write it like this

$\sqrt{81} = 9$

Questions
1. What multiple of 6 is the square root of 144?
2. What multiple of 3 is the square root of 36?

Activity
Write out the multiples of 3, up to 60. Do you recognise a pattern? Add up the digits of the multiples, e.g. 42 = 4 + 2 = 6.
Clever, don't you think?

Parent's Guide
Knowing and understanding these number facts help children to manipulate numbers, recognise number patterns and carry out mental calculations. See if your child can work out all the square roots up to 144 and check they are still practising their times tables.

Numbers

Factors/Prime Numbers

Factors

Factors are numbers that **divide into other numbers** without any remainders.

EXAMPLE:
What numbers divide into 10?

10 ÷ 1 = 10
10 ÷ 2 = 5
10 ÷ 5 = 2
10 ÷ 10 = 1

So the factors of 10 are 1, 2, 5 and 10 itself. Is 6 a factor of 10? If not, why not? What are the all the factors of 24? How about 36?

Money Fact-ors!
Our coins all represent factors of £2.00. 1p, 2p, 5p, 10p, 20p, 50p and £1.00 (which is the same as 100p) all divide evenly into £2.00 (which is the same as 200p).

Prime Numbers

Prime numbers are numbers that **cannot be divided by any number** except 1 and themselves.

2, 3, 5, 7, 11, 13, 17, 19 and 23 are all prime numbers.

Remember
1 is not a prime number.
2 is the only prime number that ends in a 2. Apart from 2 and 5 all prime numbers end in 1, 3, 7 or 9.
Prime numbers have only 2 factors; 1 and themselves.

Questions
1. What is the next prime number after 23?
2. What are the factors of 12?
3. All prime numbers are even. True or false?

Activity
Draw a number square from 1 to 100. Draw circles around all the factors of 80. Draw squares around all the prime numbers to 100, using the rules above.

Numbers

Mental Arithmetic

You have probably learnt quite a few ways of doing sums in your head at school. Here are a few reminders of some of the best methods.

Times Tables

Think of the times tables you know. If you can double numbers, this will help – you will know your 2s: 8 x 2 =16, so 8 x 4 will be double = 32. 8 x 8 will be double that = 64. Using this method you should be able to work out the calculations shown here:

Add and Subtract

- Break up numbers into smaller parts.

EXAMPLE:
78 + 39 is the same as 70 + 30 + 8 + 9.
324 – 117 is the same as 300 – 100 and 24 – 17.

Question
Complete this magic number square so that the sum of each row, column and diagonal is the same.

	1.9	
	1.8	
		1.7

Activity
Make up your own number squares and challenge a friend to complete them.

- Round up or down, then take away.

EXAMPLE:
78 + 39 can be rounded up to 80 + 40 then take away 3.
94 – 11 is the same as 94 – 10, then take away 1.

Multiply and Divide

- To multiply by 10 move the digits one place to the left and add a zero if necessary.

EXAMPLE:
3.4 x 10 = 34

H	T	U	.	tenths	hundredths
		3	.	4	
	3	4	.	0	

- To multiply by 100 move the digits two places to the left and add two zeros if necessary.

EXAMPLE:
5.6 x 100 = 560

- Dividing is the opposite: to divide by 10 move the digits one place to the right, to divide by 100 move them two places to the right.

EXAMPLE:
1.08 ÷ 100 = 0.0108

Parent's Guide
The skills involved in both mental arithmetic and calculator work are greatly improved by practice. Set your child problems they must solve in their heads and then show them how to check their answers with a calculator. Let them set you some mental calculations and see how well you do!

Numbers

Using a Calculator

In the tests one paper (Test B) allows you to use a calculator. A calculator is a useful tool – but only if you use it properly.

Tip
Always press the buttons carefully. Try and estimate the answer first; then if you have made a mistake you'll spot it.

Calculator Check List

- memory buttons
- per cent
- square root
- clear
- plus/minus
- all clear
- decimal point

- The **C** button cancels the last button you pressed. To cancel everything use the **AC** button.

- Calculators can not tell you about money or measurements. Remember to put in the pound sign and decimal point or measurement when you write the answer down.

- Pressing the **+/−** button after a number makes it a negative number.

You can find out a square root by pressing the number followed by the square root sign. You do not need to press **=**.

• To find 3% of 19:

1 **9** **x** **3** **%**

Questions
Use a calculator to find:
1. 27 % of 145
2. £47.09 x 3
3. -4.5 + 3.9

Activity
Imagine you have £100 to spend on toys. Look through a toy or mail-order catalogue and draw up your imaginary list. Use a calculator to add up the prices – see how close you can get to spending exactly £100.

25

Shape and Space

2D Shapes

2D, or two-dimensional, shapes are flat, unlike 3D shapes. They are also known as plane shapes.

Here are some examples you should learn:

Square
4 equal sides, all right angles

Rectangle
2 pairs of equal-length sides, all right angles

Rhombus
4 equal sides, no right angles
opposite sides are parallel

Parallelogram
2 pairs of equal-length sides, no right angles
opposite sides are equal

Trapezium
1 pair of parallel sides

Kite
2 pairs of equal-length sides that are adjacent
no parallel sides

Terms and Words

- A regular 2D shape has sides of equal length and equal angles.

EXAMPLE:
equilateral triangle   equilateral quadrilateral (square)

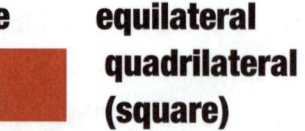

- Quadrilaterals have 4 sides.
A square, a rectangle, a parallelogram, a rhombus, a trapezium and a kite are all quadrilaterals.

- Triangles have 3 sides (see page 30)

- Polygons have straight sides. The name tells you how many:
- Pentagons have 5 sides
- Hexagons have 6 sides
- Heptagons have 7 sides
- Octagons have 8 sides

Questions
1. Draw an irregular pentagon.
2. What shape is a 20p coin?

Activity
Look up the words nonagon, dodecagon, parallel and perpendicular in a dictionary. What do they mean? Can you draw some examples of them?

Parent's Guide
Children are expected to be able to draw 2D shapes and patterns. They need to be able to describe them in terms of angles, side-lengths and parallel or perpendicular lines. Their test may require them to measure the perimeters of simple shapes and areas of rectangles.

Shape and Space

Perimeter and Area

Perimeter

The perimeter of a shape is the distance all the way round it. The perimeter of a circle is called a circumference.

You can measure the perimeter by adding up the value of all the sides:

3 cm + 3 cm + 2 cm + 2 cm = 10 cm

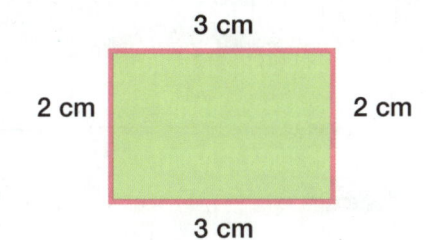

Tip
If you are not given the measurements, use your ruler.

To work out the perimeter of this shape you must calculate the missing length.

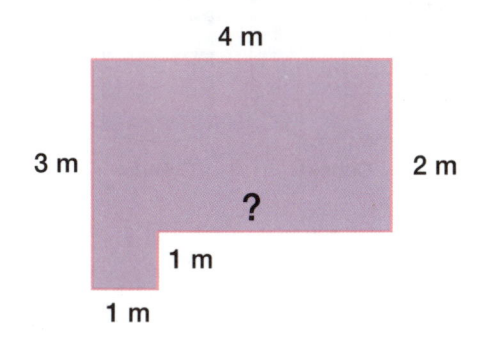

The difference between 4 m and 1 m is 3 m – so the missing length is 3 m. Now add them all together:

3 m + 4 m + 2 m + 3 m + 1 m + 1 m = 14 m

Area

You show area by putting a ² next to the measurement, e.g. 10 m², 45 cm²

To measure the area of a rectangle, measure one short side and one long side and multiply them:

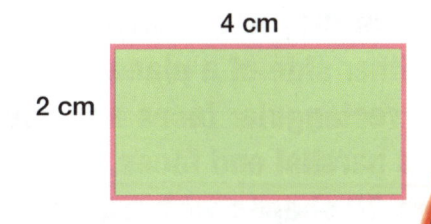

4 cm x 2 cm = 8 cm²

Questions
1. This shape is a quadrilateral. True or false?
2. What is the perimeter of this shape?
3. What is the area of this shape? (Tip: imagine it as two rectangles then add the answers.)

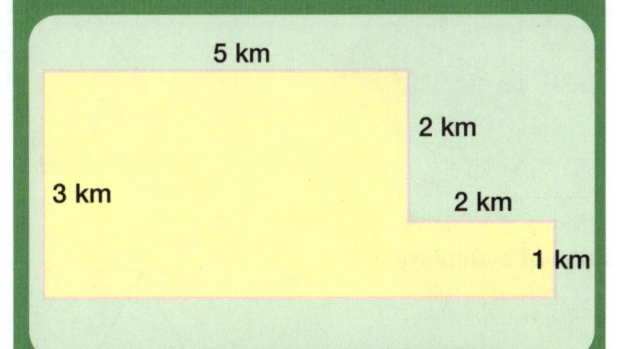

Activity
Use squared paper to draw some rectangles of different sizes. Calculate the area of the rectangles by counting the squares.

27

Shape and Space

3D Shapes

We have learnt that 2D shapes are flat. 3D shapes exist in three dimensions. Those dimensions are height, width and depth.

You need to learn that:
- 3D shapes are solid shapes.
- When you look at a picture of a 3D shape you must imagine it as a solid thing.
- 3D shapes have corners (vertices), faces and edges.
- 3D shapes can have a plane of symmetry. This means that they have mirror images on either side of a plane.
- Prisms have rectangular faces and two identical and parallel end faces.
- Pyramids are 3D shapes with triangular faces that meet at a point.

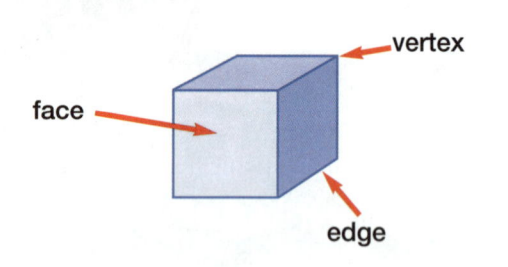

Questions
Look at the triangular prism.
1. How many vertices does it have?
2. How many faces does it have?
3. How many edges does it have?

Activity
There are 3D shapes all around you. See if you can find their planes of symmetry.

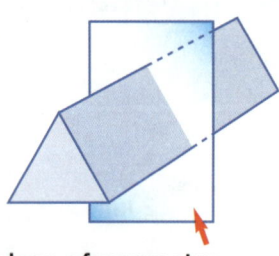

These are 3D shapes you need to know:

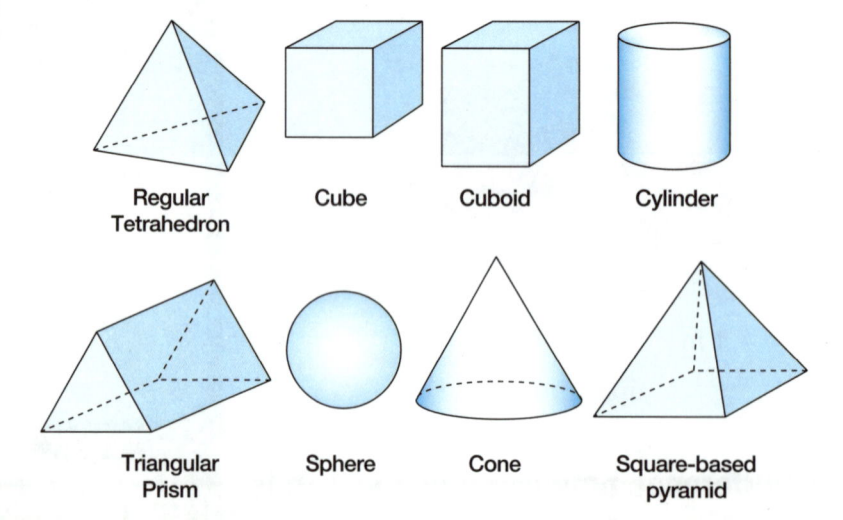

Regular Tetrahedron, Cube, Cuboid, Cylinder

Triangular Prism, Sphere, Cone, Square-based pyramid

Parent's Guide
Making 3D nets is an excellent way to understand the concept of three dimensions. Help your child measure grocery and food boxes and calculate their volumes.

Shape and Space

3D Nets and Volume

3D Nets

We can make 3D shapes using **shape nets**. These are flat shapes that we can fold and glue together to make a solid shape.

Tip
In a test, you may be asked to name the shape that a 3D net forms. There may be more than one 3D net for any shape.

Cube

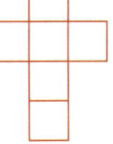

Triangular Prism

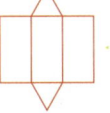

Square Based Pyramid

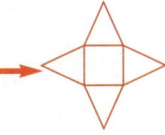

Calculating Volume

Volume is the measure of **how much space something takes up**. You should know how to measure the volume of a **cuboid**. We show volume with this symbol: ³

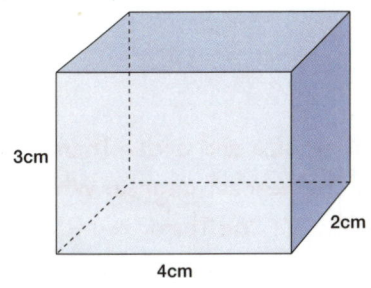

3cm
2cm
4cm
a cuboid

EXAMPLE:
15 cm^3 ('fifteen centimetres cubed').

You work volume out like this:
1. Count or measure the length, the width and the height.
2. Calculate 4 x 2 x 3
3. The answer is: 24 cm^3

Questions
1. This is a 3D net for a cube. True or false?

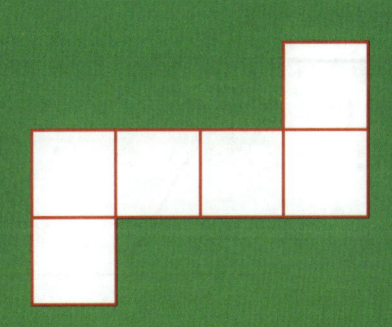

2. This is an alternative 3D net for a cuboid. True or false?

3. How many planes of symmetry does a cuboid have?

Activity
Make some of the 3D shapes shown here. You will need quite stiff paper, glue and paper clips to keep the sides in place while the glue dries.

29

Shape and Space

Angles and Triangles

Angles

Stand up and face the window. Now turn and face the door. The amount you have just turned is called an angle.

- An angle is a measure of turn.
- A full turn is 360° (three hundred and sixty degrees). Face the window then turn all the way round to face it again: you have turned 360°.
- A quarter angle is a right angle and it measures 90°.
- The angles on a straight line add up to 180° (a half angle).

EXAMPLE:

60°   120°

Triangles

Triangles are 2D shapes with three angles that add up to 180°.

Equilateral Triangle
3 sides of equal length
3 equal angles

Right-Angled Triangle
One angle is 90°

Scalene Triangle
3 sides of different lengths
3 different angles

Angles to Learn
You need to know these angles:

Acute Angle
Less than a quarter angle
<90°

Right Angle
A quarter angle
90°

Obtuse Angle
Between a quarter angle and half angle
>90° but <180°

Questions
Estimate these angles
1. ?°
2. ?°

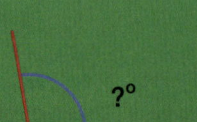

Activity
Ask a grown-up to help you use a protractor to check the accuracy of your estimates. A protractor is a tool for measuring angles.

Isosceles Triangle
2 sides of equal length
2 equal angles

Parent's Guide
Children are expected to recognise different angles, estimate their size and order them. They should be able to draw acute, obtuse and right angles to the nearest degree. When shown triangles with two angles given they should be able to calculate the third.

30

Shape and Space

Plotting Co-ordinates

We plot co-ordinates on a graph in order to be able to draw shapes accurately.

- The horizontal axis is the x-axis.
- The vertical axis is the y-axis.
- Co-ordinates are written in brackets (3,2) with the x-axis number written first.
- When you draw axes, you create four quadrants.
- The first number (x-axis) tells you how many to count across.
- The second number (y-axis) tells you how many to go up.

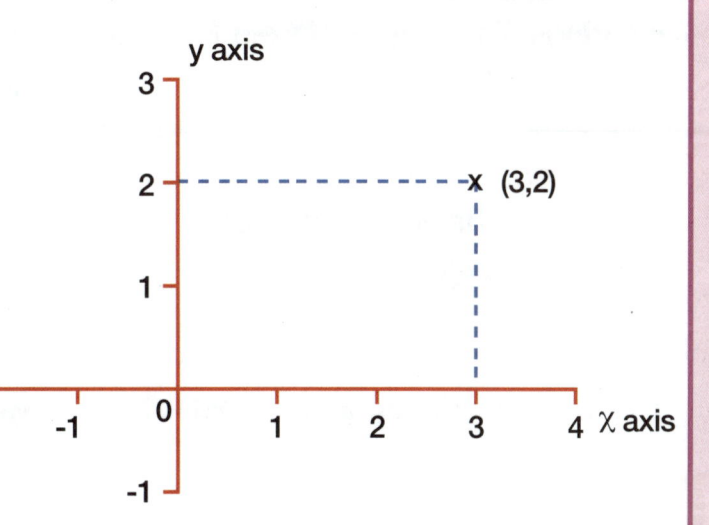

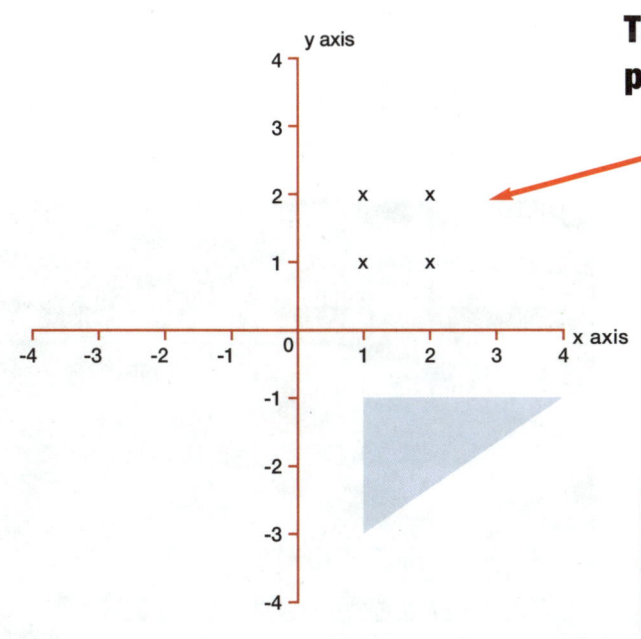

The co-ordinates for these points are: (1,1), (2,1), (1,2), (2,2)

Questions
1. Plot the points for (−2,0) (−3,1) (−3,−3) (−2,−2) on the graph to the left and then join them.
2. Name the shape you have drawn.
3. Write the co-ordinates for the blue triangle.

Activity
Ask a grown-up to teach you how to play battleships with squared paper. There is no better way to learn co-ordinates!

Remember
Go a-cross (x) the river and up the hill (y).

31

Shape and Space

Symmetry and Reflection

Two shapes that are symmetrical are identical, but they may be in different positions. There are different types of symmetry:

Reflection
This means lines of symmetry, or mirror images.

Rotation
This means rotating a shape about a point.

Translation
This means sliding or moving a shape from one place to another.

Remember
A shape may have more than one line of symmetry.

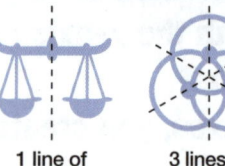

1 line of symmetry   3 lines of symmetry   No lines of symmetry

You can also reflect a shape **in a line**.

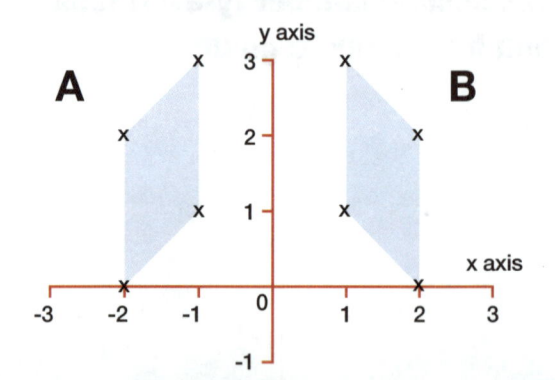

Reflection or Reflective Symmetry

You can use a mirror to work out whether a shape has reflective symmetry or not. If you can place the mirror somewhere on the shape so that the reflection – or mirror image – looks the same as it does without the mirror, you have found **a line of symmetry**.

Questions
1. Write the co-ordinates for the shape A on the graph above.
2. Write the co-ordinates for its mirror image B.

Activity
Fold a square piece of paper into 4 then cut out little shapes around the folded edges. Open out the paper and examine the pattern you have made. The folds represent lines of symmetry.

Parent's Guide
Your child was taught aspects of symmetry in Key Stage 1. Now they have to deal with the more complex concepts of rotation and translation. They need to understand how all the shapes they have been learning about can be manipulated in this way.

Shape and Space

Rotation and Translation

Rotation

Shapes that have rotational symmetry can be **turned**, or **rotated**, so they look the same.

Use a piece of tracing paper to copy the shape here. Put the tracing over the original and place a pencil point over the centre of the cross. Now turn the tracing paper. How many times does the tracing exactly match up with the original?

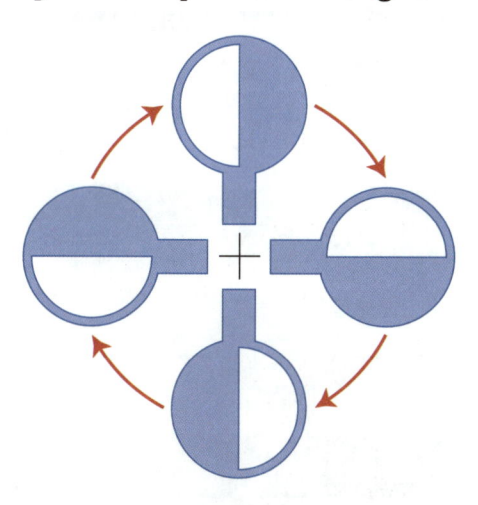

You should have been able to find 4 positions – this means the shape has **rotational symmetry of order 4**.

You can also rotate a shape about a point:

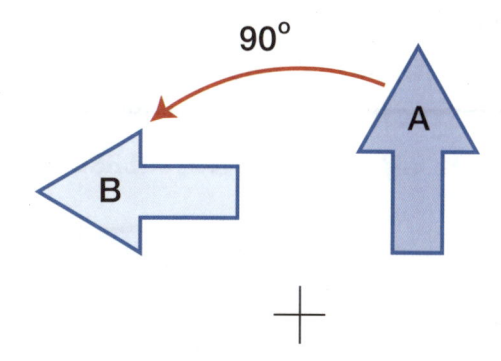

Trace this shape (A) and place the tracing over it. Place your pencil on the centre of the cross and rotate the tracing paper 90° until it covers the second shape (B).

Translation

A shape that has been translated has been moved to another place, but has not been turned at all.

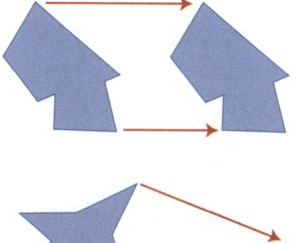

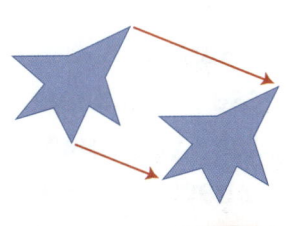

Questions
1. Name this shape
2. It has 6 lines of symmetry. True or false?
3. What is its order of rotational symmetry?

Activity
Use tracing paper to practise drawing reflections, rotations and translations on to graph paper.

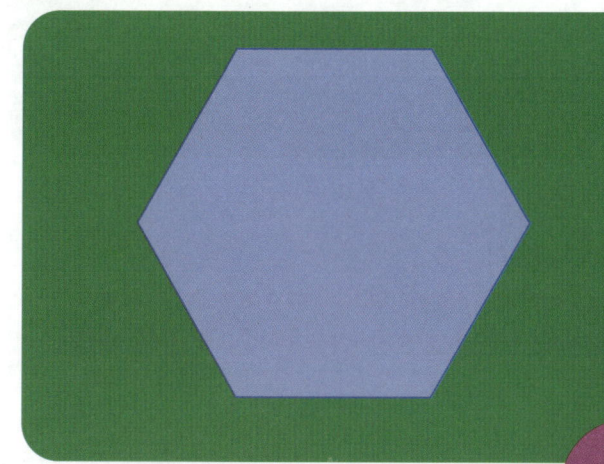

Handling Data

Measuring

When you measure you need to know two things:
- The units of measurement, e.g. litres, centimetres, hours, pounds etc.
- What instrument is being used to measure, e.g. ruler, watch, measuring jug etc.

Units

You must know:
10 mm = 1 cm
100 cm = 1 m
1000 m = 1 km
1000 ml = 1 l
1000 g = 1 kg
- Area is measured in squared units e.g. cm^2 m^2 km^2
- Volume is measured in cubed units e.g. cm^3 m^3 km^3

Instruments

Measuring instruments have scales. These are the numbers that you read to take your measurement. Sometimes you have to work out numbers that are not written in:
EXAMPLE:
Look at this centimetre ruler. The reading here would be 70 cm.

Time – What You Need to Know

- How to read an analogue clock (with a face and hands) and a digital clock (where the time is in figures).
- All the units of time, e.g. seconds, minutes, hours, days, weeks, months, years, decades and centuries.
- a.m. means 'before midday' (12 noon) and p.m. means 'after midday'.
- How to tell the time using the 24-hour clock (1 a.m. is 01:00 in the 24-hour clock and 1 p.m. is 13:00).

Questions
1. Read these scales. Remember to state what the units are.

2. Put these times into the 24-hour clock:
a. A quarter past eleven in the morning.
b. 12.03 p.m.

Activity
Look at the train timetable at your local station. Can you work out how long certain journeys take? You need to remember that an hour has 60 minutes in it.

Parent's Guide
When children learn to measure, tell the time and understand simple statistics they understand how mathematics applies to everyday life. This offers parents a great opportunity to talk about maths and explain its relevance by using real examples.

Handling Data

Tables and Charts

We have just revised measurements – now we can remind ourselves of some of the best ways to **record** those measurements.

Tallying

Tallying is a method of keeping score: it tells us about **frequency** – how often something has happened. The results can be displayed in a table. A **table** is a good way of displaying information.

Three children throw a dice. Every time someone throws a 6 it is marked on the **frequency table**. A line is drawn for each 6. The fifth line crosses the previous four. The totals are then written down too, to make the results easier to read.

Name	Tally	Total
Sam	ⅢⅠ ⅠⅠ	7
Amy	ⅢⅠ ⅢⅠ	10
Tom	ⅢⅠ ⅢⅠ ⅠⅠⅠ	13

Pie Charts

Pie charts are used to show information. They are based on a circle, and **proportions** are shown as segments of the circle. Go back to pages 20 and 21 if you need to remind yourself about proportions.

EXAMPLE:
During Numeracy Hour Mrs Davis spends:
- A third of the lesson on mental maths.
- Half of the lesson writing on the blackboard.
- One sixth of the lesson telling children to be quiet.

Remember
- If you make a pie chart using fractions they must all add up to 1.
- If you use percentages they must add up to 100%.

Questions
The table below shows the favourite flavour ice cream for 36 children. Not all of it has been filled in.

FLAVOUR	TALLY	NUMBER
Vanilla		12
Chocolate	ⅢⅠ ⅠⅠⅠ	
Strawberry	ⅠⅠⅠⅠ	
Mint		6
Rum 'n' raisin	ⅢⅠ	

1) Fill in the missing information.
2) How many children preferred chocolate ice cream?
3) Which flavour was most popular?
4) Could you convert this information into a graph or pie chart?

Activity
Make a frequency chart with the numbers 1 to 6 down the side. Throw a dice 100 times and mark the frequency for each number, using the tallying method. Write down the totals for each number.

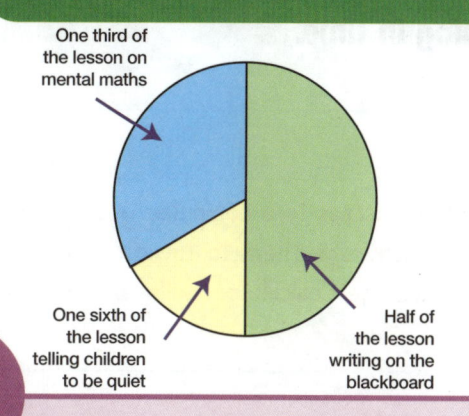

One third of the lesson on mental maths

One sixth of the lesson telling children to be quiet

Half of the lesson writing on the blackboard

Handling Data

Bar Charts/Line Graphs

Bar Charts

We use bar charts to show information because they are easier to understand than lists of numbers.

EXAMPLE:
This chart shows the most popular fruits in Year Five's lunchboxes one Tuesday.

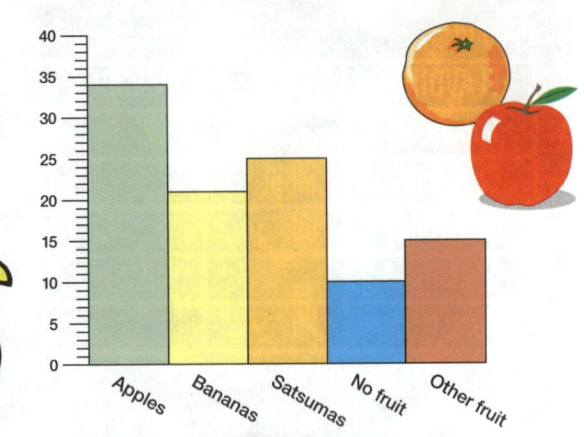

Remember
Time is always put on the horizontal axis.

EXAMPLE:
This graph shows the amount of rain that fell in the first 6 months of a year.

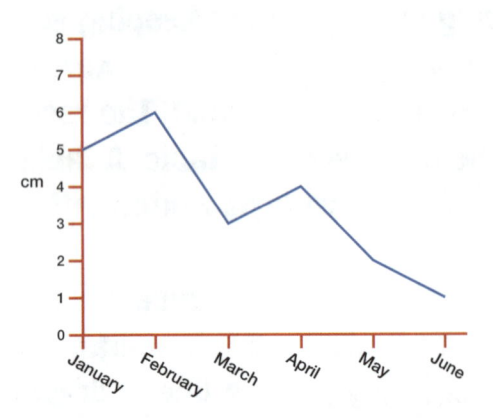

Between which two months did the rainfall decrease the most?

Line Graphs

Line graphs show information, too. They use points, plotted on graph paper, instead of bars. Look at page 31 again to remind yourself about plotting co-ordinates.

Line graphs are often used to give information about things that are happening in time.

Questions
Look at the bar chart and line graph.
1. How many lunchboxes were checked in total?
2. January was the wettest month. True or false?

Activity
On page 35 you made a frequency chart for throwing a dice. Use those totals to draw a bar chart. Put the numbers (1 to 6) along the bottom and the frequency up the side.

Parent's Guide
If you have access to a computer you can show your child how to draw tables, graphs and charts using it. Encourage them to try different methods of showing the same information. Children can practise their calculator skills to work out averages.

Handling Data

Averages and Probability

Averages

We use **averages** to give us more information than we can get from just looking at numbers or graphs. **Mode**, **median** and **mean** are all types of average.

EXAMPLE:
15 children were asked how many siblings (brothers and sisters) they had. This is a **frequency** table of their results.

Number of siblings	Frequency
6	1
5	1
4	2
3	2
2	3
1	2
0	4

- The **mode** is the result that occurs **most often**. Here it is 0 because 0 has a frequency of 4 – higher than any other number of siblings.
- When the information – or data – is written down in order of size, the **median** is the **middle number**.
  0 0 0 0 1 1 2 2 2 3 3 4 4 5 6
  The median number is 2.
- To find the **mean** add up all the values then divide by the total number of values (15).
  0 + 0 + 0 + 0 + 1 + 1 + 2 + 2 + 2 + 3 + 3 + 4 + 4 + 5 + 6 = 33
  33 ÷ 15 = 2.2
  The mean is 2.2

Probability

Probability means 'how likely something is to happen'. This number line shows how we might measure probability.

- 0%   will definitely not happen
- 25% unlikely
- 50% might happen, might not
- 75% likely
- 100% will definitely happen

We can describe probability – or **chance** – as a number. If Sam throws a piece of buttered toast up in the air it can land one of two ways: on the plain side or on the buttered side. We say it has a **1 in 2 chance** of landing on the buttered side because it will land **1 of 2 possible ways**.

Questions
1. How many numbers are there on a dice?
2. What is the probability that you will throw a 5?
3. What is the probability you will throw an even number?

Activity
On page 35 you were asked to make a frequency chart for throwing a dice 100 times. Look at your chart and see how it compares with the probabilities you have just calculated.

37

Practice Papers

Introduction to Practice Test Papers

The National Tests

Children at the end of Key Stage 2 (Year 6) take tests in English, maths and science. Each subject in the National Curriculum is divided into core subjects. In mathematics, for example, these are:
- Number
- Shape, Space and Measures
- Handling Data

Targets are set for achievement within these core subjects. In mathematics, for example, 'Number' includes:
- Using and Applying Numbers e.g. problem-solving
- Numbers and the Number System e.g. fractions
- Calculations e.g. mental arithmetic

A combination of written tests, (SATs) and continuous classroom assessment enables the teachers to record the targets individual children have met.

What do SATs Involve?

The children are given written papers to complete. In mathematics they have three or four papers:
- Tests A and B are each 45 minutes long and are taken by all children. A calculator may be used in Test B. Both tests are used to assess Levels 3–5 (see below).
- Test C is 30 minutes long and a calculator is allowed. It is used to assess children who are working at Level 6. Your child is unlikely to take Test C: it is given to children who are expected to achieve Level 5 easily and are working at an exceptional level in mathematics.
- The Mental Arithmetic Test is taken by all children. Twenty questions are read out to the children who use their mental maths skills to answer them. The answers are written on a specially prepared answer sheet.

Introduction

How are National Tests Marked?

Children sit the exams in May and the test papers are sent away for marking. Results come back in July.

- Most children will achieve results between Level 3 and Level 5.
- Level 3 indicates that extra work is required to reach the target for this age group.
- Level 4 indicates that targets set for this age group have been attained.
- Level 5 or above indicates that the targets for their age group have been exceeded.
- Generally, children are expected to move up one level every two years.

What are National Test Results Used For?

SATs results may indicate several things:
- Whether a child is progressing through the levels appropriately.
- Whether a school is doing well.
- Areas of weakness that a child might need extra help with.
- Test results may also be used, with other assessments, to help Year 7 teachers decide how to allocate children to suitable ability groups or classes.

How Should I Use the Practice Papers?

In this section of the book you will find examples of all four types of test. Your child should not attempt to take any of the tests until they have, at least, skimmed through the revision section and answered the questions they encountered on the way.

It can be de-motivating to do badly in a test. Ensure your child has a good understanding of the concepts and techniques used in each practice paper before they attempt it.

Encourage your child to complete a practice test paper in real exam conditions. This means no help, no breaks and only the equipment allowed in the instructions to the test.

Answers are in the back of the book. It is essential that you help your child to correct any mistakes they make. Heap plenty of praise on them for the work they complete correctly and reward them for good corrections that are done promptly.

If your child continues to struggle with a subject you should discuss this with their teacher, who may be able to suggest an alternative way of helping them.

Practice Papers

Test 1

Instructions

You **may not** use a calculator to answer any questions in this test.

You have **45 minutes** for this test.

Work as quickly and carefully as you can.

If you cannot do one of the questions, go on to the next one. You can come back to it later, if you have time.

If you finish before the end, go back and check your work.

Follow the instructions for each question carefully.

This shows you where you need to put the answer.

If you need to do working out, you can use any space on a page.

1 MARK

This box shows the number of marks available for each question or part of a question.

Some questions have a box like this one to write your answers in.

Show your working. You may get a mark

Test 1

2 MARKS

1. Draw lines to join the circle to two more number cards which make 175.

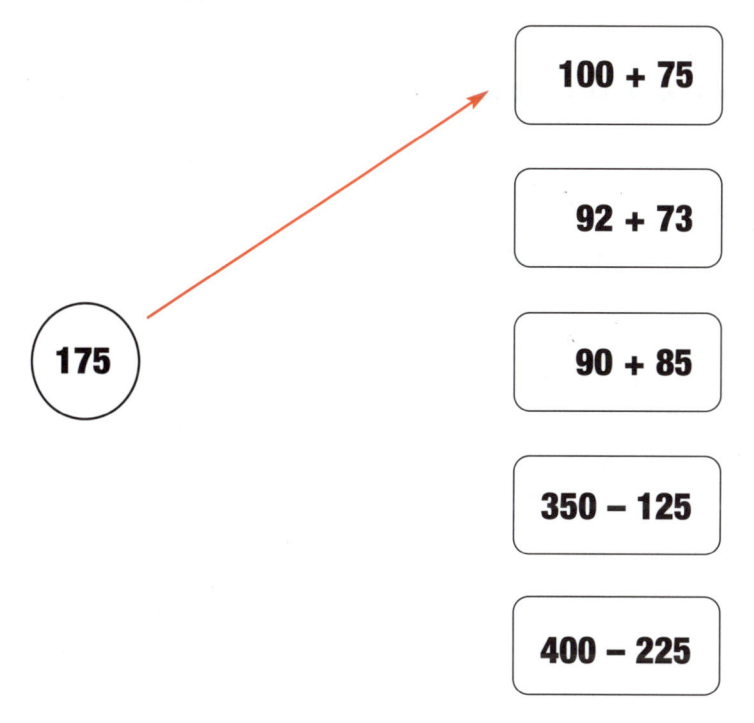

   175

   100 + 75

   92 + 73

   90 + 85

   350 − 125

   400 − 225

1 MARK

2. Write in the missing numbers.

   7 x 50 = ☐

1 MARK

   8 x ☐ = 200

Practice Papers

3. Here is a rectangle with a pattern on it.

The rectangle is reflected in the mirror line.

Draw the missing square and dots on the reflected rectangle.

You may use a mirror or tracing paper.

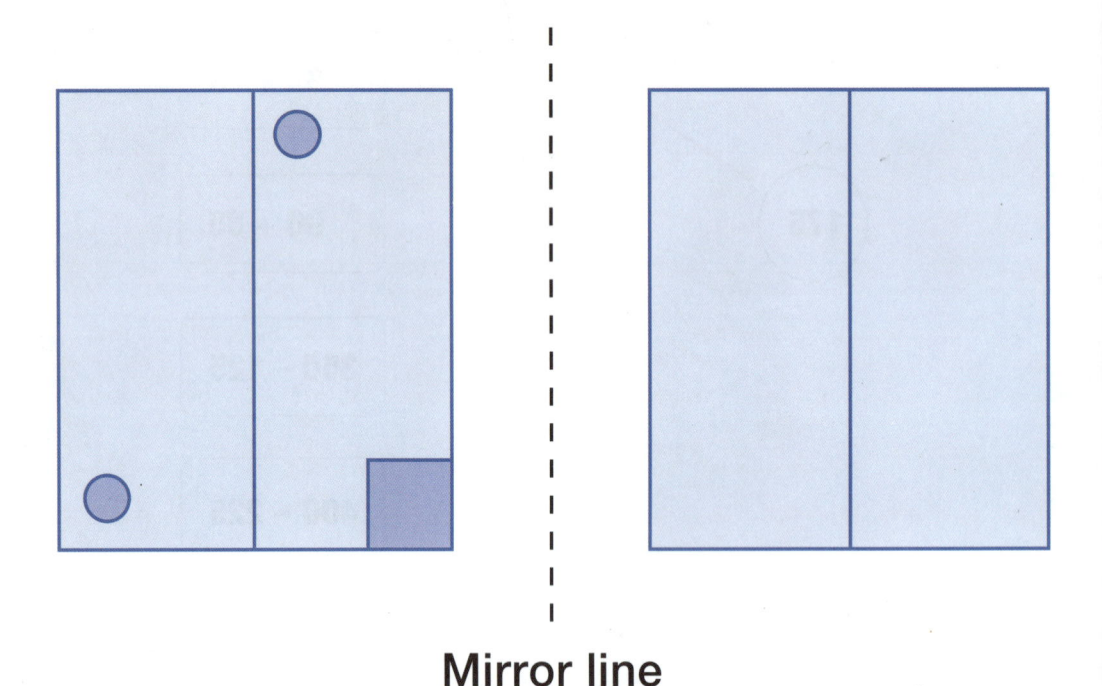

1 MARK

Mirror line

4. Nneka, Adele and Bob go to the shops by tram.

This is what they pay:

Nneka   95p

Adele   £1.80

Bob   £2.10

a) How much more does Bob pay than Nneka?

1 MARK

42

1 MARK

Adele leaves the shops and gets the bus to visit her Granny in hospital. She pays 45p for her bus ticket.

b) How much has Adele paid **altogether** for her two tickets?

2 MARKS

5. Match each shape on the left to one with equal area on the right.

One has been done for you.

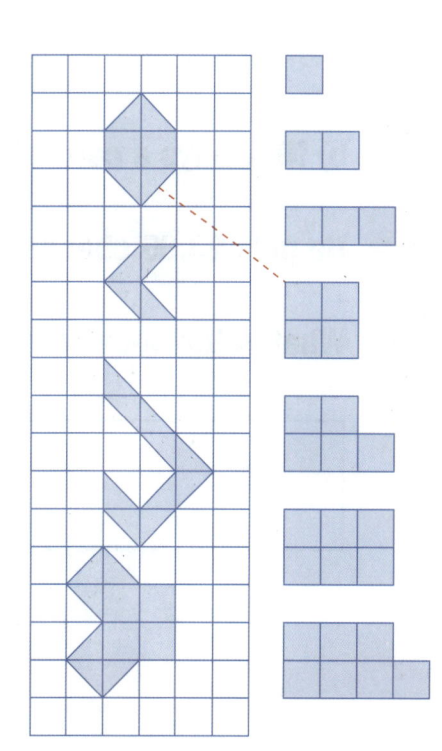

43

Practice Papers

6. A shop sells greetings cards. Each card has a price code printed on the back.

These are the codes:

CODE	PRICE
AA	85p
BB	£1.25
CC	£1.45
DD	£1.60
EE	£1.95

a) Jonny buys three cards.

1 MARK

One has code AA on it, one has code BB and one has code CC.

How much does Jonny pay?

b) Nick buys a card. He pays with a £5.00 note.

1 MARK

He gets £3.05 change.

What is the code on his card?

Test 1

7. Circle all the multiples of 9 in this list of numbers.

1 MARK

18   35   45   53   62   81

8. Tick (✓) two cards that give a total of 6.

1 MARK

$1\frac{1}{4}$ $2\frac{1}{4}$ $1\frac{3}{4}$

$3\frac{1}{2}$ $3\frac{3}{4}$ $4\frac{1}{4}$

9. Choose 3 of these number cards to make an even number that is greater than 420.

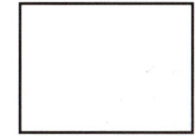

1 MARK

1   7   8   3

45

10. This graph shows the cost of going on the Internet in the daytime and in the evening.

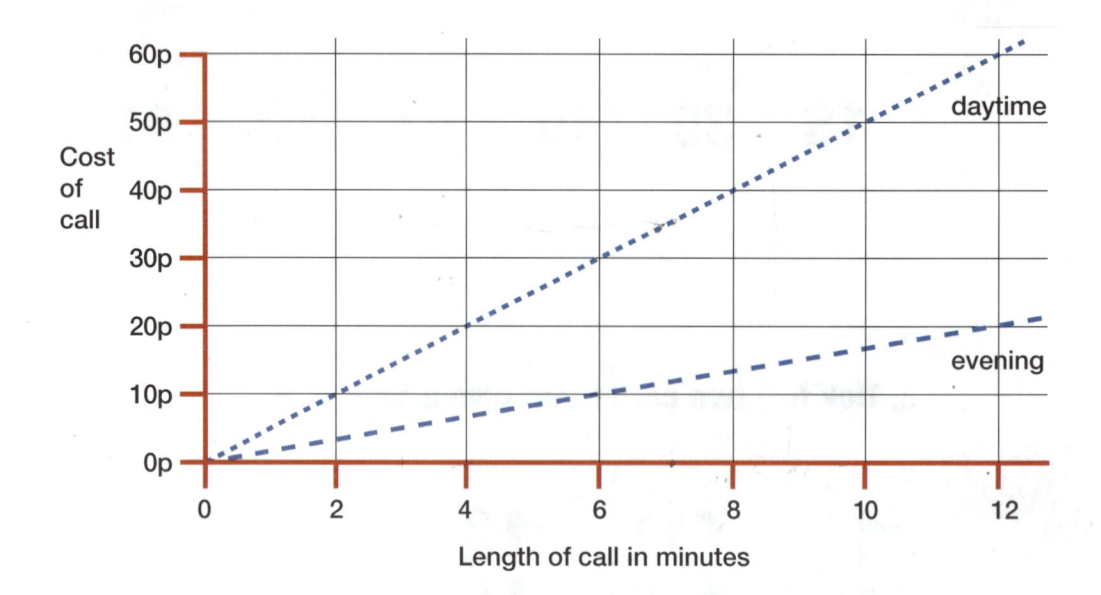

a) How much does it cost to go online for **7 minutes** during the **daytime**?

1 MARK

b) How much **cheaper** is it to go online for **6 minutes** in the evening than in the daytime?

1 MARK

46

11. Mr Roberts has decided to make a mural for the classroom wall. He buys coloured paper and silver paper for the border.

Paper

£1.75 per sheet
silver paper 50 cm x 50 cm

£3.25 per sheet
coloured paper 100 cm x 50 cm

a) He buys 4 sheets of coloured paper and 4 sheets of silver paper.

What is the total cost of the paper he buys?

Show your working. You may get a mark.

2 MARKS

b) Mr Roberts tells the class: 'It would cost more to use silver paper all the way round.'

Explain why he is correct.

1 MARK

Practice Papers

12. Write in the missing digits

3 [ ] 6 + 2 5 [ ] = 6 3 1

1 MARK

13. Here is a slice of Neapolitan ice cream.

| Vanilla | Strawberry | Chocolate |

0 1 2 3 4 5 6
centimetres

a) What is the length of the whole slice?

Give your answer in millimetres

1 MARK

b) What is the length of the strawberry section of ice cream?

Give your answer in millimetres

1 MARK

14. Calculate 517 x 30

1 MARK

48

Test 1

2 MARKS

15. This table shows the weight of some cooking ingredients.

Complete the table.

	grams	kilograms
flour	2500	2.5
butter		0.75
sugar	500	
cocoa powder		0.05

1 MARK

16. Calculate 17.09 – 13.72

1 MARK

17. The shaded area below is a parallelogram.

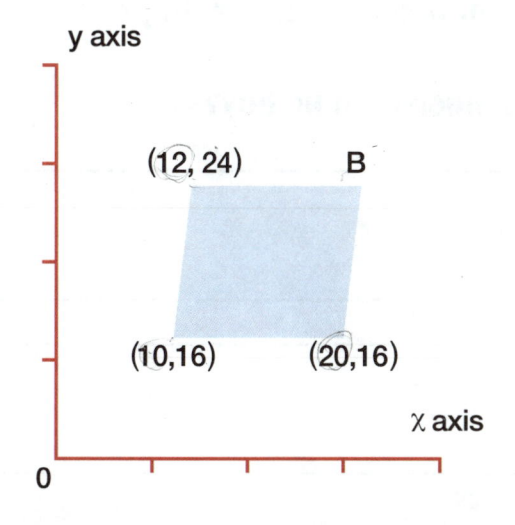

y axis

(12, 24)   B

(10, 16)   (20, 16)

x axis

0

1 MARK

Write in the co-ordinates of point **B**

( ), ( )

49

Practice Papers

18.

7 tomatoes for 80p   10 onions for 75p

Marek bought some packets of tomatoes and bags of onions.

He spent £3.90

2 MARKS

a) How many **packets** of tomatoes did he buy?

b) How many **bags** of onions did he buy?

Show your working. You may get a mark

packets of **tomatoes**:

bags of **onions**:

1 MARK

c) Which is cheaper, one tomato or one onion?

Show your working. You may get a mark

50

1 MARK

19. Write in the **two** missing digits.

[ ][0] x [ ][0] = [3][5][0][0]

2 MARKS

20. A sequence starts at 450 and 75 is subtracted each time.

450   375   300 …

The sequence continues in the same way.

Write the first two numbers in the sequence which are less than zero.

Practice Papers

2 MARKS

21. Michael has a bag of 8 counters numbered 1 to 8.

Anna has a bag of 20 counters numbered 1 to 20

Each chooses a counter from their own bag without looking.

For each statement put a tick (√) if it is true or a cross (x) if it is not true.

Michael is more likely than Anna to choose a 6

a

They are both equally likely to choose a number less than 4

b

Michael is more likely than Anna to choose an even number

c

Anna is more likely than Michael to choose a 10

d

2 MARKS

22. Calculate 918 ÷ 27

Show your working. You may get a mark

23. Look at this diagram

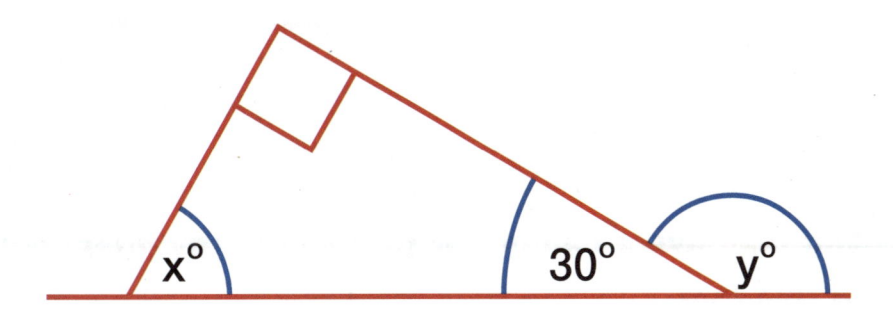

x°   30°   y°

Calculate the size of angle x and angle y.

Do not use a protractor (angle measurer).

1 MARK   x = [   ]°

1 MARK   y = [   ]°

24. Which is larger, $\frac{2}{3}$ or $\frac{4}{5}$?

Explain how you know.

1 MARK

Practice Papers

Test 2

Instructions

You **may** use a calculator to answer any questions in this test.

You have **45 minutes** for this test.

Work as quickly and carefully as you can.

1 MARK

1. Circle **3** numbers which **add** to make **170**

   10   30   60   80   70

1 MARK

2. Write in the missing number:

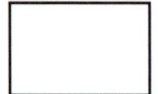

   ☐ x 6 = 360

1 MARK

3. Shade in **two or more squares** to make this design symmetrical about the mirror line.

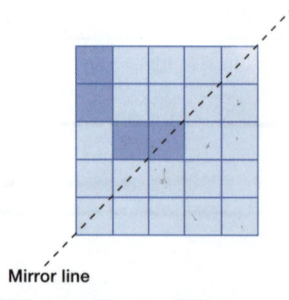

   Mirror line

   You may use a mirror or tracing paper.

54

Test 2

4. Write in what the missing numbers could be.

   (☐ ÷ ☐) + 50 = 75

5. This chart shows the after-school clubs that some children attend.

	Jerome	Joanna	Sunita	Adrian	Kujo
drama	✓	✓		✓	
chess	✓		✓		
Irish dancing		✓		✓	
football	✓	✓			✓
choir			✓		

a) Who goes to both drama and Irish dancing?

b) How many children attend more than two after-school clubs?

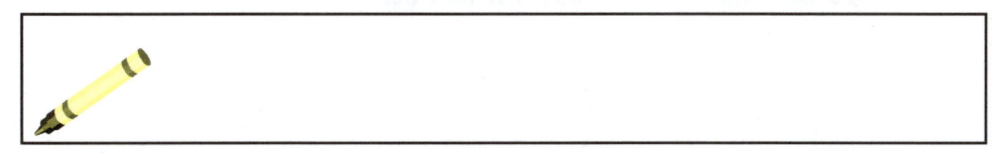

6. Pencils are sold in boxes of 20

a) Mrs. Hughes buys 8 boxes of pencils. How many pencils is this?

b) Mr Stewart needs 180 pencils. How many boxes does he need to buy?

55

Practice Papers

2 MARKS

7. Here are some number cards

| 3 | 3 | 3 |

| 8 | 8 | 8 |

Use 5 of the number cards to make this correct

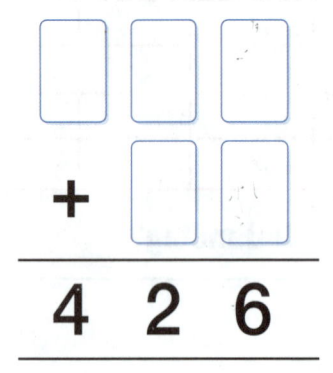

```
  ☐ ☐ ☐
+   ☐ ☐
───────
  4 2 6
```

8. Tania makes this shape from four cubes stuck together.

Two circles are painted on the shape.

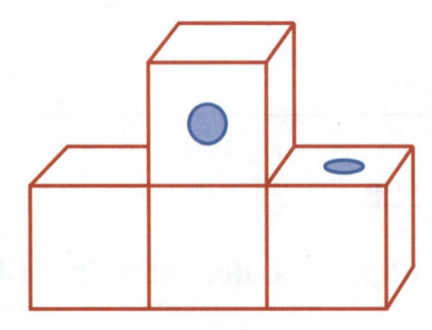

Tania moves the shape.

Draw the circles on the shape in its new position.

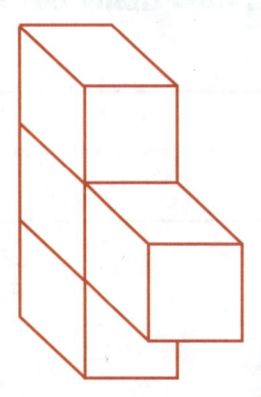

1 MARK

56

9.

Bike Hire	
Mountain Bikes	Quad Bikes
£1.75 for 1 hour	£3.50 for 1 hour

a) How much does it cost to hire a mountain bike for 2 hours?

1 MARK

b) Sophie hires a quad bike at 2.40 p.m. and she pays £7.00. By what time must she return?

1 MARK

10. Circle two numbers which have a difference of 3.

1 MARK

-2   -1.5   -1   -0.5   0   0.5   1

Practice Papers

11. This is the cost of going swimming.

| Adults | £4.10 |
| Children | £2.80 |

2 MARKS

a) On Saturday morning 10 adults and 12 children go swimming. How much do they pay altogether?

Show your working. You may get a mark

Armbands costs £1.75 per pair.

The swimming pools sells £7.00 worth of armbands.

1 MARK

b) How many pairs of armbands is this?

Test 2

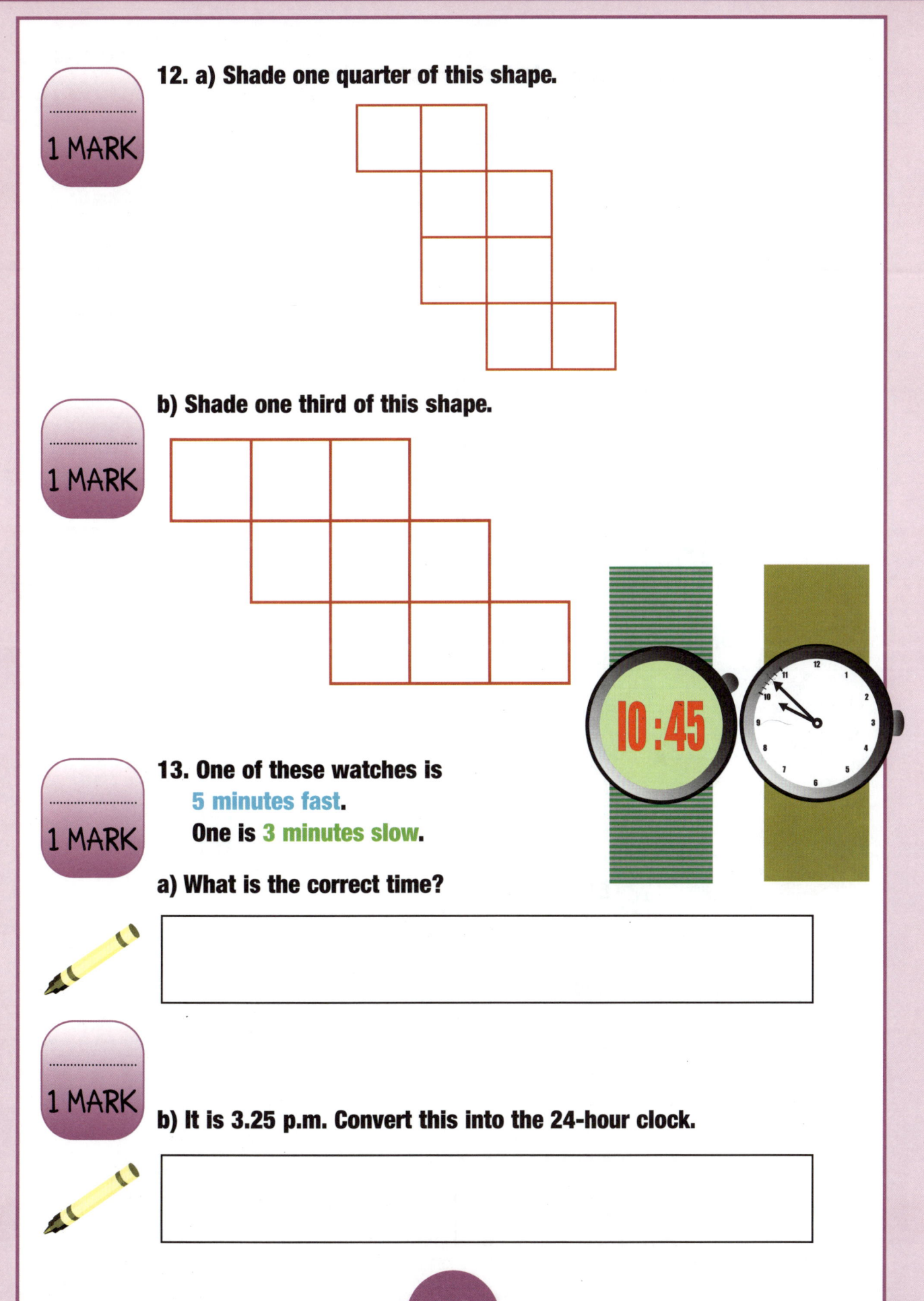

12. a) Shade one quarter of this shape.

1 MARK

b) Shade one third of this shape.

1 MARK

13. One of these watches is
   5 minutes fast.
   One is **3 minutes slow**.

1 MARK

a) What is the correct time?

1 MARK

b) It is 3.25 p.m. Convert this into the 24-hour clock.

59

Practice Papers

14. Match each box to the correct number.

One has been done for you.

$\frac{1}{6}$ of 180	40
	15
	25
$\frac{1}{2}$ of 40	30
	10
	20
$\frac{1}{3}$ of 45	35

1 MARK

15. Here are 5 shapes on a square grid.

1 MARK

Which **two** shapes fit together to make a **rectangle**?

and

60

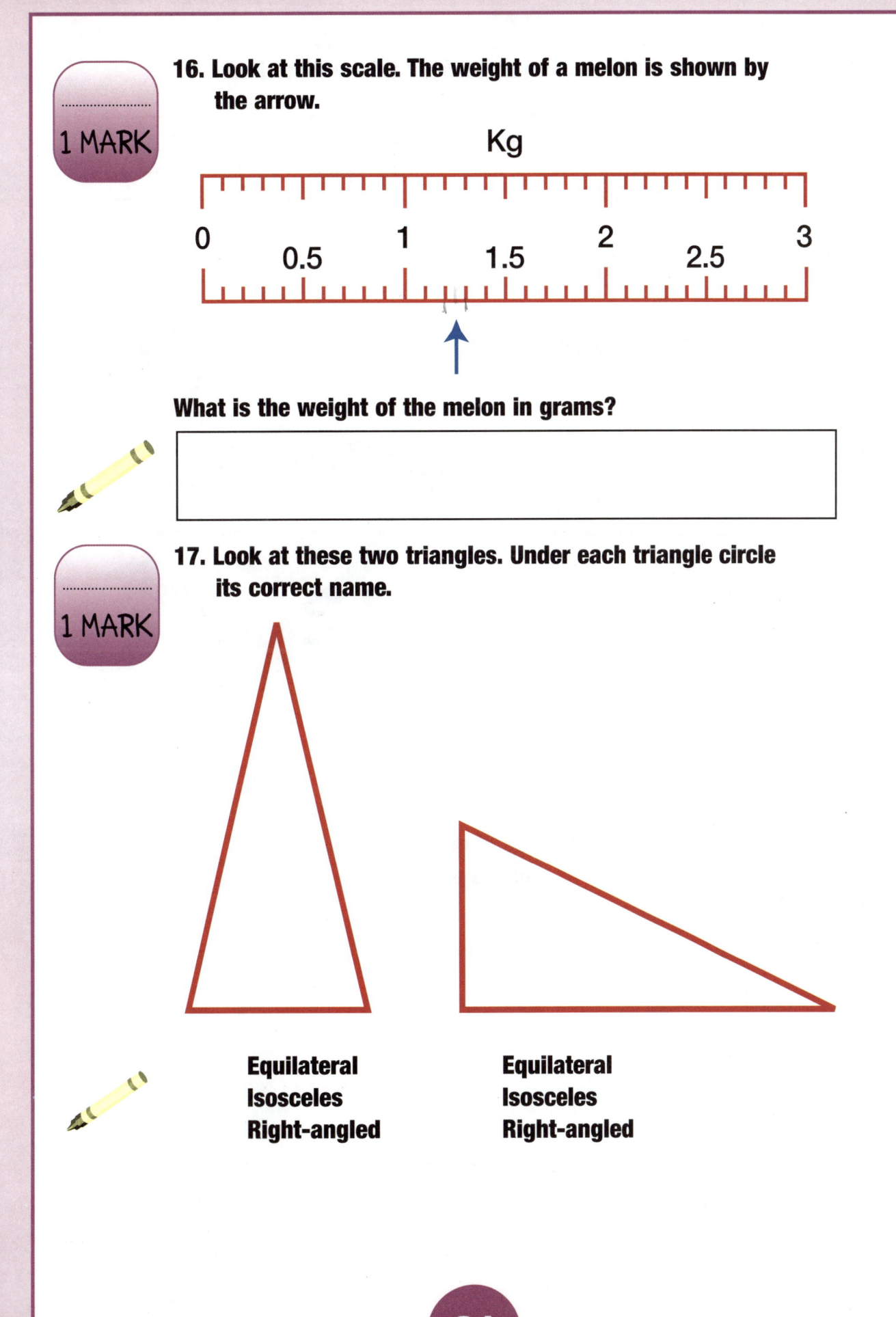

16. Look at this scale. The weight of a melon is shown by the arrow.

Kg

0   0.5   1   1.5   2   2.5   3

What is the weight of the melon in grams?

1 MARK

17. Look at these two triangles. Under each triangle circle its correct name.

1 MARK

Equilateral
Isosceles
Right-angled

Equilateral
Isosceles
Right-angled

Practice Papers

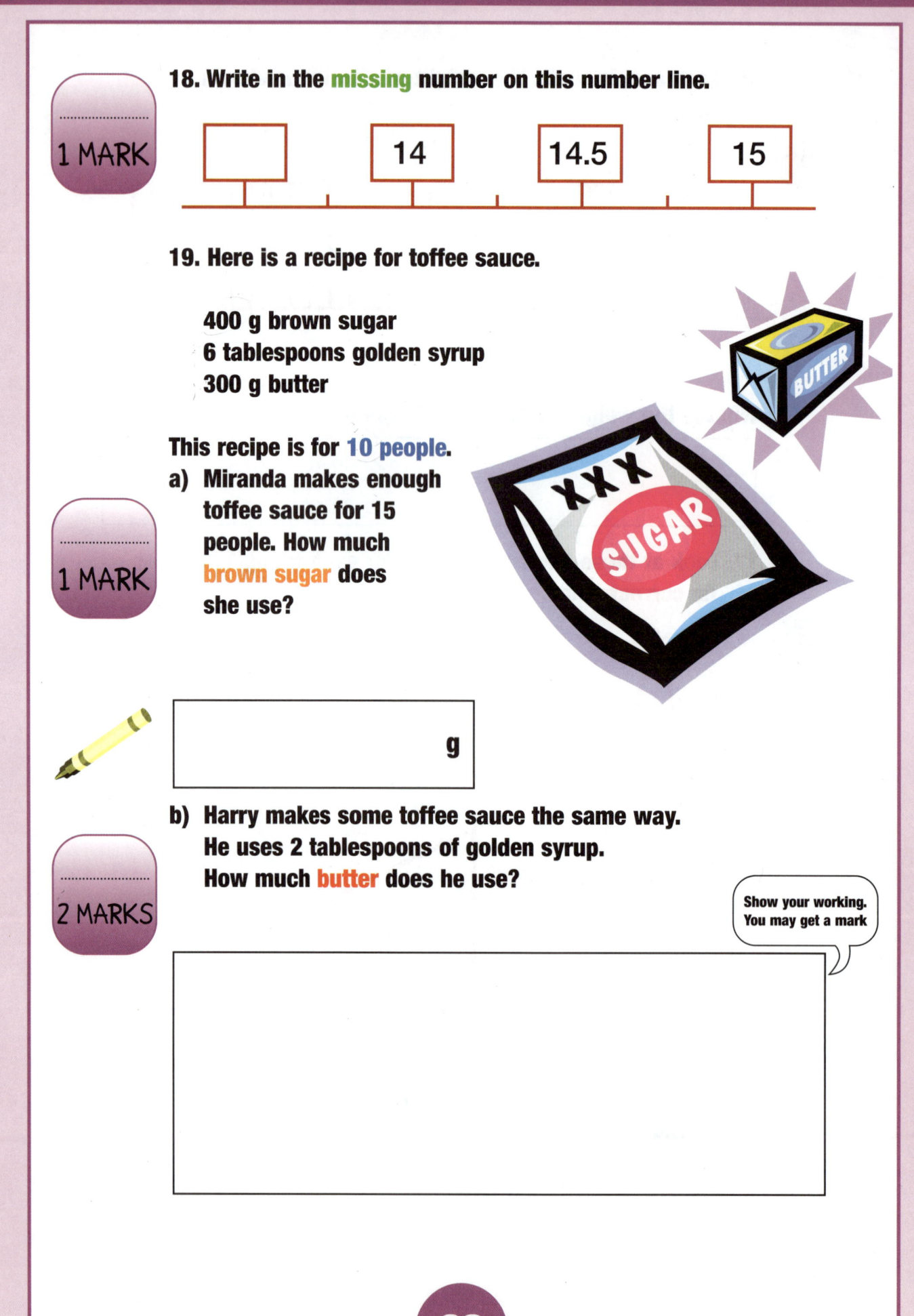

18. Write in the missing number on this number line.

1 MARK

| ☐ | 14 | 14.5 | 15 |

19. Here is a recipe for toffee sauce.

400 g brown sugar
6 tablespoons golden syrup
300 g butter

This recipe is for 10 people.

a) Miranda makes enough toffee sauce for 15 people. How much **brown sugar** does she use?

1 MARK

☐ g

b) Harry makes some toffee sauce the same way.
He uses 2 tablespoons of golden syrup.
How much **butter** does he use?

2 MARKS

Show your working. You may get a mark

Test 2

20. Holly makes this shape with a **rectangle** and an **equilateral triangle**. The measurements of the rectangle are shown.

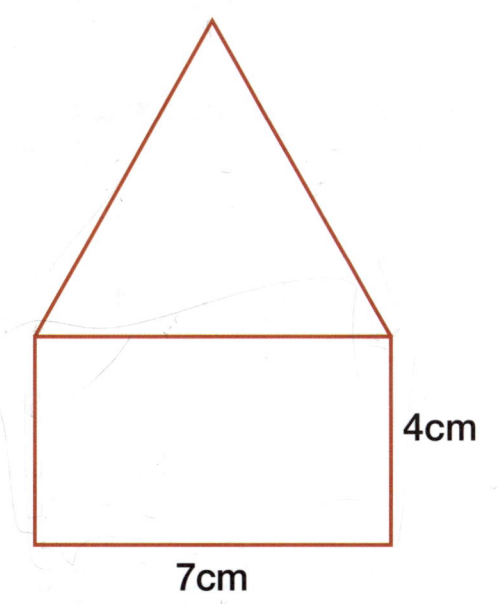

4cm

7cm

Not actual size

Calculate the perimeter of this shape without using a ruler.

☐ cm

1 MARK

21. Write in the missing number.

462.72 ÷ ☐ = 48.2

1 MARK

22. Write the 3 prime numbers which multiply to make 105.

☐ × ☐ × ☐ = 105

1 MARK

Practice Papers

1 MARK

23. The rule for this sequence of numbers is 'add 4 each time'.

1   5   9   13   17   21   25 …

Katie says 'You can keep going on in this sequence forever, but there will never be a multiple of 4 in the sequence.'

Is Katie right?
Circle yes or no   Yes   /   No

Explain how you know

_____

_____

_____

_____

1 MARK

24. Calculate 18% of 256.

25. A cup of tea is left to cool down. This graph shows how the temperature of the tea changes as it cools.

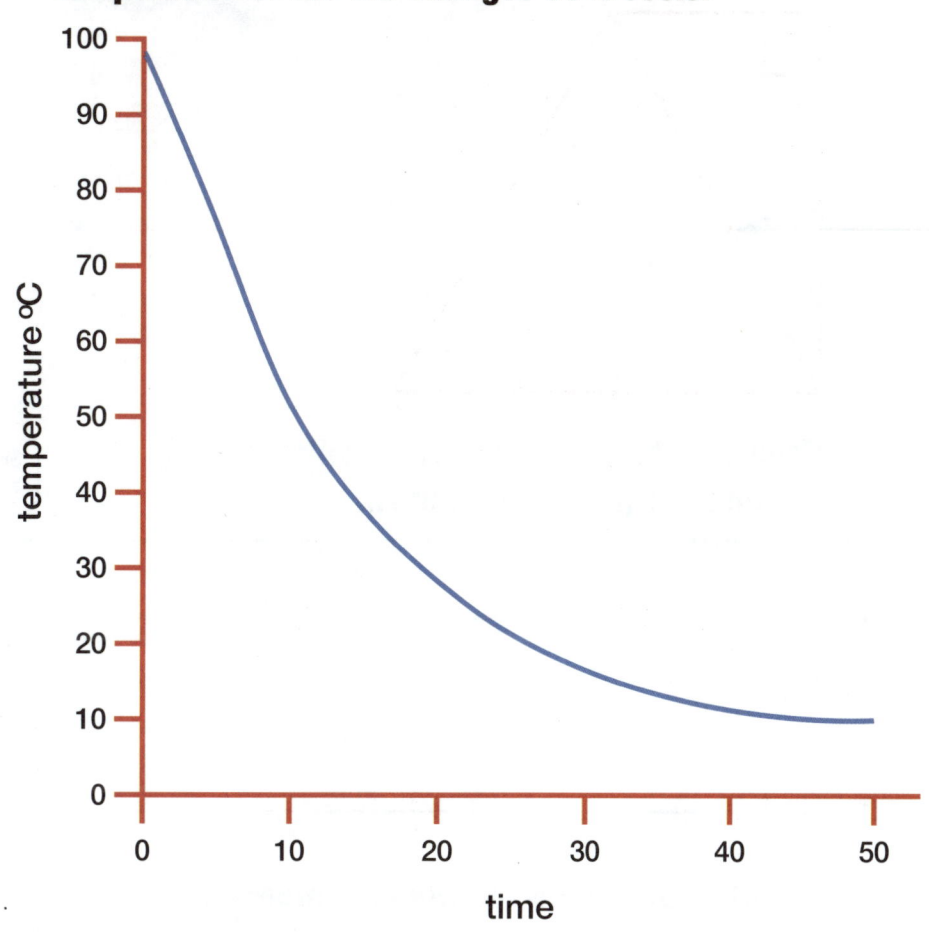

Look carefully at the graph.

a) What temperature is the tea after 25 minutes?

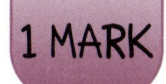

⬚ °

b) Read from the graph how many minutes it takes the tea to cool from 95° to 80°.

⬚ minutes

Practice Papers

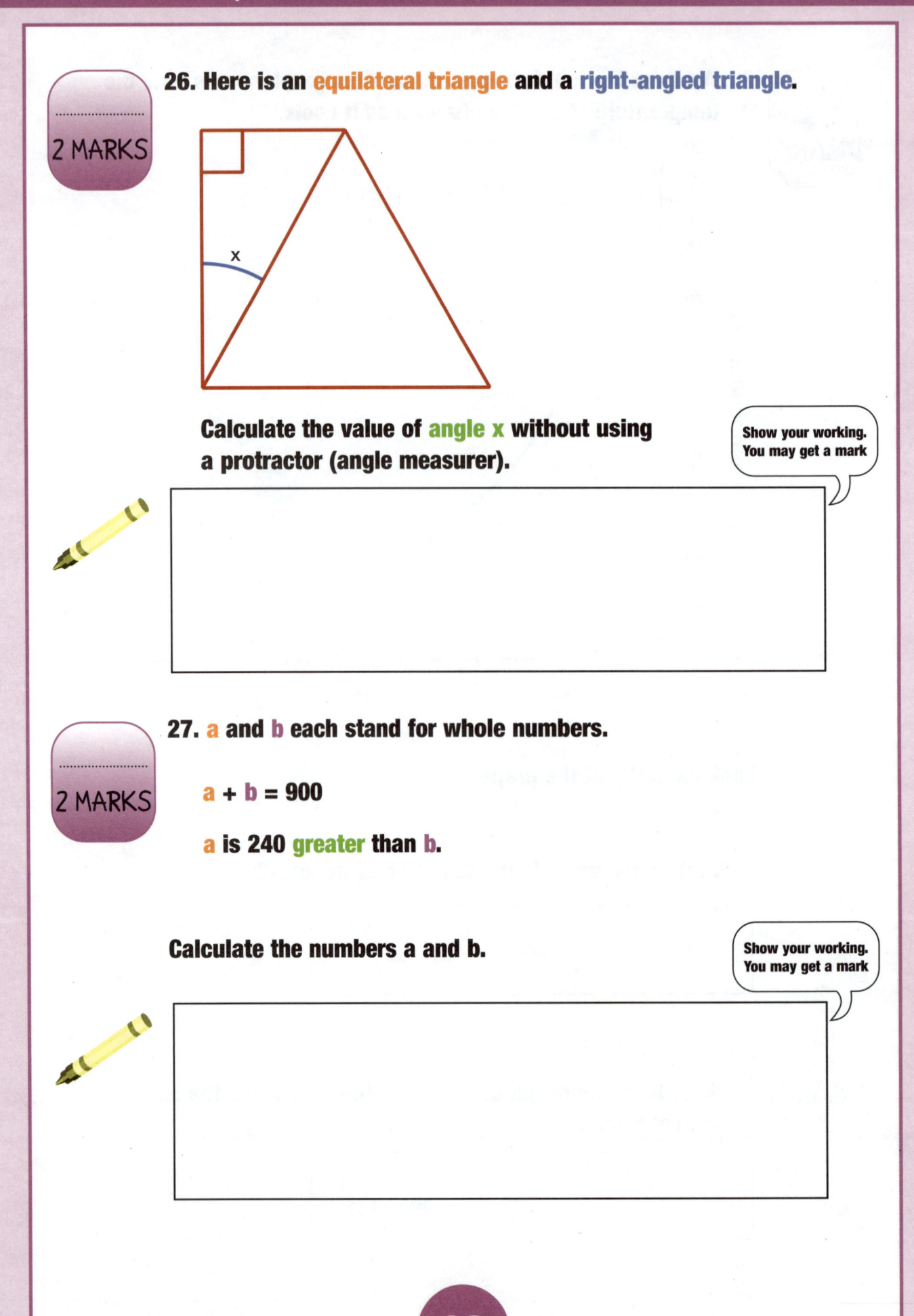

26. Here is an **equilateral triangle** and a **right-angled triangle**.

2 MARKS

Calculate the value of **angle x** without using a protractor (angle measurer).

Show your working. You may get a mark

27. **a** and **b** each stand for whole numbers.

2 MARKS

a + **b** = 900

a is 240 **greater** than **b**.

Calculate the numbers a and b.

Show your working. You may get a mark

Test 3: Mental Arithmetic

Instructions

You will find a sheet where the answers are to be written on page 79. Please detach this before starting the test. This is for you to write on. You should only use pens or pencils. Do not use rulers, rubbers, calculators or any mathematical equipment. You are not allowed to use any paper for working out. If you want to change an answer cross it through then write your correction clearly. You need to ask an adult or a friend to read the questions out to you.

Instructions to the Tester or Parent

You need to have a clock or watch that measures seconds accurately.

Read the following instructions to the child.

Listen carefully to the instructions I am going to give you. When I have finished reading them, I will answer any questions. However, you will not be able to ask any questions once the test has begun.

I will start by reading a practice question. Then I am going to ask you 20 questions for the test. On your sheet there is an answer box for each question, where you should write the answer to the question and nothing else. You should work out the answer to each question in your head, but you may jot things down outside the answer box if this helps you. Do not try to write down your calculations because this will waste time and you may miss the next question. For some of the questions, important information is already written down on the sheet.

I will read out each question twice. Listen carefully both times. You will then have time to work out your answer. If you cannot work out an answer put a cross. If you make a mistake, cross out the wrong answer and write the correct answer next to it. There are some easy and some harder questions, so don't be put off if you cannot answer a question.

Here is the practice question to show you what to do. I will read the question twice, and you will have 5 seconds to work out the answer and write it on the dotted line.

What is 34 add 8?

Repeat the question.

Wait five seconds then read out the following:

Now put down your pencil.

Check that the child has written the answer in the correct place, then you can begin the test.

Practice Papers

Mental Arithmetic Test

> For this group of questions you will have 5 seconds to work out each answer and write it down.

1. Add fifty-six and eighty.
2. Write in figures the number four thousand and sixty-three.
3. Multiply nine by four.
4. What is the square root of 49?
5. What is 30 multiplied by 200?

> For the next group of questions you will have 10 seconds to work out each answer and write it down.

6. Look at the table on your answer sheet. What is the cost of 3 kg of limes?
7. What is the time fifteen minutes after ten fifty?
8. Subtract two hundred and ten from three hundred.
9. What is the sum of seven point four and seven point seven.
10. Look at the shapes on your answer sheet. Put a tick in the shape which is a pentagon.
11. Look at your answer sheet. Put a ring around the fraction which is equal to nought point six.
12. An equilateral triangle has a perimeter of twenty-four centimetres. How long is one of its sides?
13. Ten times a number is seventy-four. What is the number?
14. Calculate the difference between three hundred and seventy-four and four hundred and twenty-six.
15. What is ninety per cent of two hundred?

> For the next group of questions, you will have 15 seconds to work out each answer and write it down.

16. Add together fifty-two, fifty-five and fifty-eight.
17. Jasmine thought of a number. She doubled it and added three. The answer was sixty-seven. Which number did she think of?
18. Look at your answer sheet. Put a ring around the number which is not a factor of five hundred.
19. What is two thousand divided by twenty?
20. Five tulips cost one pound fifty. How much do fifteen tulips cost?

Now put down your pen or pencil. The test is finished.

Test 4: Level 6

> You **may** use a calculator in this test.
> You have 30 minutes for this test.

1 MARK

1. This number sequence follows the rule
   'Subtract 5, then divide by 10'

   ☐   115   11   0.6   ☐

   Write the **two numbers** missing from this sequence.

1 MARK

2. Write **two decimals, each less than 1**, which multiply to make **0.2**.

   ☐ x ☐ = 0.2

1 MARK

3. This 4-digit number is a square number. Write in the missing digits.

   | 9 | | | 9 |

Practice Papers

1 MARK

4. The diagram shows 1 shaded **equilateral triangle**.

(Not to scale)

Calculate the size of the angle x and the angle y.

Do not use a protractor (angle measurer)

x = ☐   y = ☐

5. Find the **value of x** in this equation.

8 + 3x = 80 − 9x

1 MARK

6. Mr Harrold's factory produces approximately **690 million** staples each year.

Next year he hopes to **increase this by 23 million**.

2 MARKS

a) Use this information to **calculate the percentage** increase in the amount of staples the factory will produce next year.

Show your working. You may get a mark

2 MARKS

b) Mr Harrold says, 'an increase of 23 million staples each year is more than **43 staples each minute**'.

Show that he is correct

Show your working. You may get a mark

70

Test 4

7. Here are two sequence of numbers.

x	y
6	2
8	3
10	4
12	5

a) What will the value of x be when y = 50?

Show your working. You may get a mark

2 MARKS

b) What is the rule connecting x and y?

1 MARK

8. A cuboid has a square base.
It is twice as tall as it is wide.
Its volume is 128 cubic centimetres.

Not actual size

Calculate the width of the cuboid.

Show your working. You may get a mark

2 MARKS

Practice Papers

2 MARKS

9. This diagram shows **4 identical shaded triangles** in a rectangle.

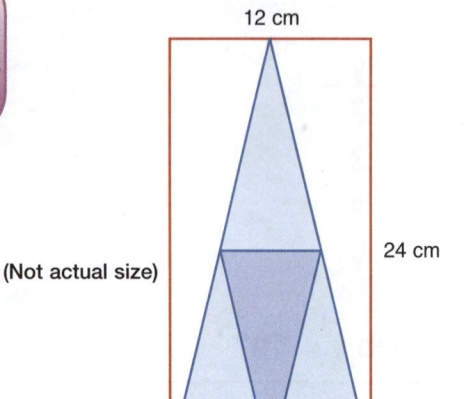

12 cm

(Not actual size)

24 cm

The rectangle measures 12 cm by 24 cm

Calculate the area of one shaded triangle.

Show your working. You may get a mark

2 MARKS

10. A stands for a **multiple of 4**.
    B stands for a **different multiple of 4**.
    Tick (✓) each statement according to whether it is **always true**, **sometimes true** or **never true**.

	always true	sometimes true	never true
The sum of A and B is a multiple of 8			
The difference between A and B is a multiple of 4			
The product of A and B is a multiple of 16			

1 MARK

11. The diagram shows the graph of
    $y = x - 3$
    Write the **co-ordinates** of one point on the line between A and B

    (⬚ , ⬚)

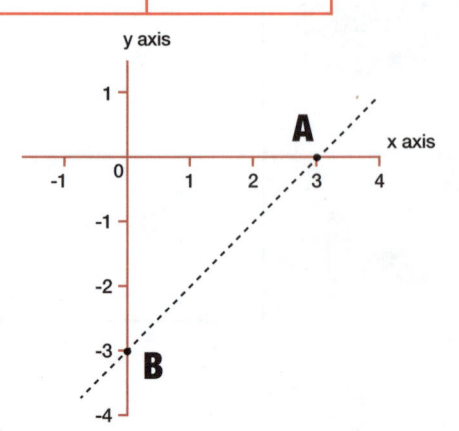

72

Test 4

2 MARKS

12. Betty counts the number of baked beans in 10 cans.

She works out that the **mean** number of baked beans in a can is 148. Here are the results for **9 cans**.

Number of baked beans in a can:

145	146	147	148	149	150
✓	✓	✓	✓	✓	✓
	✓			✓	✓

Calculate how many beans are in the **tenth can**.

Show your working. You may get a mark

2 MARKS

13. The diagram shows 6 **shaded squares**
    B is the point (10, 5)

What are the co-ordinates of A and C?

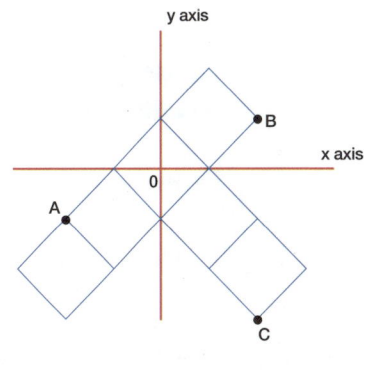

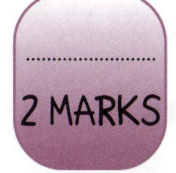

A = (_____ , _____)]

C = (_____ , _____)]

2 MARKS

14. In a survey, the **ratio** of the number of adults who preferred **tea** to those who preferred **coffee** was **7:4**.

69 more people preferred tea to coffee.

How many people were in the survey?

Show your working. You may get a mark

73

Glossary

Here are some important words you should try and learn before your test. Cover up the words and test yourself on the meanings.

Acute Angle	Less than 90°
Congruent	The same
Cube Numbers	The result of a single number being multiplied by itself three times
Denominator	The number at the bottom of a fraction
Equilateral triangle	3 sides of equal length, 3 angles of 60° each
Equivalent Fractions	Fractions that look different but mean the same thing
Even Numbers	Numbers that divide by 2
Factors	Numbers that divide into something
Integer	A whole number
Inverse	Opposite
Isosceles Triangle	2 sides equal, 2 angles equal
Mass	How heavy something is
Mean	An average that is worked out by adding all the numbers then dividing by how many numbers there are
Median	An average that is worked out by selecting the middle number
Mixed Fractions	Fractions and whole numbers together e.g. $6\frac{1}{2}$
Mode	An average that is worked out by selecting the most frequent number
Numerator	The number at the top of a fraction
Obtuse angle	More than 90°
Odd Numbers	Numbers that give a remainder when divided by 2
Per cent	Out of a hundred
Perimeter	The distance all the way around the outside of a plane (flat) shape
Prime Numbers	Numbers that do not divide by anything except 1 and themselves
Probability	How likely something is to happen
Range	The difference between the largest and the smallest number
Reflex angle	More than 180°
Right angle	90°
Right-angled triangle	1 angle of 90°
Rotational symmetry	Turning a shape into different positions so it looks the same
Scalene triangle	3 sides different, 3 angles different
Shape Net	A plan of a 3D shape
Square Numbers	The result of a number being multiplied by itself
Square Root	The number that is multiplied by itself to give a square number
Translation	Sliding a shape without turning it
Vertices	Corners
Vertex	One corner
Volume	The space something takes up

Test 1
Answers and Marking Scheme

1. 90 + 85; 400 − 225
   Award one mark for each correct line drawn.

2. a) 350; b) 25
   Award one mark for each correct answer.

3. Award one mark. Shading not necessary.

4. a) £1.15; b) £2.25
   Award one mark for each. Can be shown in pence or pounds.

5. Award two marks for three shapes correctly matched. Award one mark for any two shapes correctly matched.

6. a) £3.55; b) EE
   Award one mark for each correct answer.

7. 18, 45 and 81 should all be circled.
   Award one mark. Do not award the mark if additional numbers are circled.

8. $2\frac{1}{4} + 3\frac{3}{4}$ or $1\frac{3}{4} + 4\frac{1}{4}$
   Award one mark for either combination.

9. 718 or 738
   Award one mark for either.

10. a) 35p
    Award one mark for answer in the range 34p to 36p inclusive.
    b) 20p
    Award one mark for 20p or £0.20.

11. a) £20
    Award two marks for correct answer. Award one mark if correct working out but incorrect answer.
    b) An explanation which recognises that one piece of coloured paper is cheaper than two pieces of silver paper can be awarded one mark, e.g. calculations that show that it would cost £21, e.g. 'Two times £1.75 is £3.50, which is more than £3.25'.

12. 376 + 255 = 631
    Award one mark for the correct answer.

13. a) 58 mm or 5 cm 8 mm; b) 24 mm or 2 cm 4 mm
    Award one mark for each correct answer.

14. 15 510
    Award one mark for the correct answer.

15. The table should be completed as below:

	grams	kilograms
flour	2500	2.5
butter	750	0.75
sugar	500	0.5
cocoa powder	50	0.05

    Award two marks if exactly correct; one mark if two numbers are completed correctly.

16. 3.37
    Award one mark for the correct answer.

17. (22, 24)
    Award one mark for co-ordinates written in correct order.

18. a) 3 packets of tomatoes; 2 bags of onions
    Award two marks for the correct answers, one mark if the answers are incorrect but appropriate working is shown.
    b) One onion is cheaper.
    Award one mark for the correct answer and working which shows that the price per unit for an onion is less than for a tomato.

19. Accept either 50 x 70 = 3500 or 70 x 50 = 3500
    Award one mark for the correct answer.

20. -75 in the first box; -150 in the second box
    Award one mark for each correct answer.

21. Award two marks for boxes ticked or crossed as here: ✓ ✗ ✗ ✓
    Award two marks for the correct answers. Award one mark if three out of four are correct.

22. 34
    Allow two marks for correct answer. Allow one mark for correct working but incorrect answer. Correct working may include long division, short division (as long as carrying figures are evident) or repeated subtraction and addition methods etc.

23. x = 60°; y = 150°
    Award one mark for each. If answers are correct but transposed award one mark only.

24. An appropriate explanation should be awarded one mark.
    E.g $\frac{2}{3} = \frac{10}{15}$ and $\frac{4}{5} = \frac{12}{15}$ so $\frac{4}{5}$ is larger.
    E.g $\frac{2}{3} = \frac{4}{6}$ which is smaller than $\frac{4}{5}$.
    No mark awarded for correct answer alone.

Test 2
Answers and Marking Scheme

1. 30, 60 and 80 should be circled.
   Award one mark.

2. 60
   Award one mark.

3. One mark for shading squares as shown.

4. Award one mark for any pair of numbers with quotient 25 (they must be in the correct order).

5. a) Joanna and Adrian; b) 2
   Award one mark for each correct answer (both names must be given to earn the full mark).

6. a) 160; b) 9
   Award one mark for each correct answer.

7. 338
   + 88
   = 426
   Award two marks for correct answer. Award one mark if incorrect answer but eights have been placed in both unit columns.

8. One mark for both circles on faces as shown.

9. a) £3.50; b) 4.40 p.m. (accept 'twenty to five' or 16:40)
   Award one mark for each correct answer.

10. -2, 1
    Award one mark for getting both numbers correct.

11. a) £74.60
    Award two marks for correct answer. One mark if answer incorrect but evidence of appropriate method.
    b) 4
    Award one mark for correct answer.

12. a) Award one mark for any two squares shaded;
    b) Award one mark for any three squares shaded.

13. a) 10.48; b) 15:25
    Award one mark for each correct answer.
    Ignore a.m. or p.m.

14. ($\frac{1}{3}$ of 45) should be joined to 15; ($\frac{1}{6}$ of 180) should be joined to 30.
    Award one mark for the diagram completed correctly.

15. A and E
    Award one mark for both.

16. 1250 g
    Award one mark. (Ignore g)

17. Isosceles; right-angled
    Award one mark for both correctly circled.

18. 13.5
    Award one mark.

19. a) 600 g
    Award one mark. Ignore 'g'.
    b) 100 g
    Award two marks for correct answer, even if calculation not shown. Award one mark for correct working but incorrect answer.

20. 29 cm
    Award one mark.

21. 9.6
    Award one mark.

22. 3, 5, 7
    All three are required for the one mark.

23. 'Yes' should be circled. The explanation should show that every number is one more than a multiple of four. Award one mark. No mark is awarded for circling 'yes' alone.

24. 46.08
    Award one mark.

25. a) Award one mark for answer in the range 18–22° inclusive; b) Award one mark for range of 3 to 5 minutes inclusive.

26. x = 30°
    Award two marks for correct answer. Award one mark for incorrect answer but correct working which recognises that all angles in an equilateral triangle are 60° and that angles in a right angle equal 90°.

27. a = 570; b = 330
    Both answers must be correct for two marks to be awarded. Award one mark for answers in wrong order or one mark for incorrect answers but correct working that shows, for example:

    b + b + 240 = 900
    b + b = 660
    b = 330
    a = 900 − 330 = 570

Test 4
Answers and Marking Scheme

1. The first box should contain 1155; the second box should contain -0.44.
   Award one mark for each.

2. Award one mark for any combination of decimals, less than one with the sum of 0.2, e.g 0.4 x 0.5; 0.25 x 0.8.

3. 9409
   Award one mark.

4. a) $x = 65°$; b) $y = 75°$
   Award two marks for correct answers. If answers incorrect but method demonstrates that the sum of angles in a triangle and straight line each equal 180° award one mark.

5. $x = 6$
   Award two marks for correct answer, award one mark if incorrect but method shows correct algebraic manipulation.

6. a) 3.33%
   Award two marks. Award one mark if answer incorrect but correct calculation is demonstrated, e.g. 23 ÷ 690 x 100.
   b) Award two marks for calculation that shows 43.76 staples would be produced per minute. Award one mark for calculation that shows 23 000 000 ÷ 365 ÷ 24 ÷ 60.

7. a) 102
   Award two marks. For incorrect answer award one mark if calculation shows 50 x 2 +2.
   b) $x = 2y + 2$
   Award one mark.

8. 4 cm
   Award two marks. Award one mark for incorrect answer but correct method which shows: n x n x 2n = 128
   n x n x n = 64.

9. 36 cm²
   Award two marks. One mark for evidence alone:
   e.g. 12 x 24 = 288
   $\frac{288}{2}$ = area of 4 triangles = 144
   $\frac{144}{4}$ = 36 cm²

10.
	always true	sometimes true	never true
The sum of A and B is a multiple of 8		✓	
The difference between A and B is a multiple of 4	✓		
The product of A and B is a multiple of 16		✓	

   Award two marks for three correct answers, one mark for two out of three.

11. Award one mark for any co-ordinates on the line, e.g. (2,-1) (1, -2) (1.5, -1.5) etc.

12. 149
    Award two marks. If incorrect answer award one mark if correct working is shown, e.g. 148 x 10 = 1480 so tenth can must be 1480 less (145 x 1) + (146 x1) + (147 x 2) etc.

13. a) A = (-10, -5); b) C = (10, -15)
    Award one mark for each.

14. 253
    Award two marks. For incorrect answer but accurate method award one mark, e.g. 69 ÷ 3 x 11

Answers: Test 3 & Revision Guide Questions

Mental Arithmetic Test
1. 136
2. 4063
3. 36
4. 7
5. 6000
6. £2.55
7. 11:05
8. 90
9. 15.1
10. The pentagon should be ticked
11. The circle should be around $\frac{6}{10}$
12. 8
13. 7.4
14. 52
15. 180
16. 165
17. 32
18. The circle should be around 45
19. 100
20. £4.50

Revision Guide Questions

Page 6
1. Eight thousand two hundred and ninety-seven, ten thousand and four, five hundred and fourteen, nine hundred and ninety-nine.
2. a) 7; b) 4; c) 2
3. a) 70; b) 9000

Page 7
1. 24
2. 1145
3. 2794
4. a) 224; b) 44; c) 72

Page 8
1. 324
2. 2832

Page 9
1. 14
2. 5
3. 18

Page 10
1. 9000
2. £116.12

Page 11
1. 128
2. 36
3. 91

Page 12
1. 20, 70, 100, 120
2. 700, 1800, 600

Page 13
1. 38p
2. 40p
3. Six

Page 14
1. 1, 4, 9, 16, 25, 36, 49, 64, 81, 100
2. 1, 8, 27, 64, 125, 216

Page 15
1. -311 < -10 < -1 < 0 < 2 < 16 < 45 < 208
2. 4
3. A whole number

Page 16
1. $+1\frac{1}{2}$
2. $-1\frac{1}{2}$

Page 17
1. $\frac{4}{8}$
2. $\frac{2}{8}$
3. $\frac{7}{8}$

Page 18
1. -1.9, 0.01, 2.4, 7.02, 7.2, 9.76
2. 1, 2, 2, 104

Page 19
1. 8.38
2. -122.05
3. 0.625, 0.75, 0.15

Page 20
1. 26
2. 52
3. 13

Page 21
1. 7:10
2. 3:10
3. 3:7

Page 22
1. 12
2. 6

Page 23
1. 29
2. 1, 2, 3, 4, 6, 12
3. False

Page 24
1. This is just one possible solution

1.9	1.1	2.4
2.3	1.8	1.3
1.2	2.5	1.7

Page 25
1. 39.15
2. £141.27
3. -0.6

Page 26
1. Your drawing should be of a 5-sided figure with unequal sides
2. Heptagon

Page 27
1. False
2. 20 km
3. 17 km^2

Page 28
1. 6
2. 5
3. 9

Page 29
1. True
2. True
3. 3

Page 30
1. 45°
2. 100°

Page 31
1. You should have drawn a trapezium
2. Trapezium
3. (1, -1) (4, -1) (1, -3)

Page 32
1. (-1,1) (-2,0) (-2,2) (-1,3)
2. (1,1) (2,0) (2,2) (1,3)

Page 33
1. Hexagon
2. True
3. 6

Page 34
1. 1.75 kg
2. a) 11:15; b) 12:03

Page 35
1. Vanilla: |||| |||| ||; Chocolate: 8; Strawberry: 4; Mint: |||| |; Rum 'n' raisin: 5
2. 8
3. Vanilla

Page 36
1. 105
2. False. February was.

Page 37
1. 6
2. 1 in 6
3. 3 in 6, which is the same as 1 in 2

Mental Arithmetic Test

~Practice question ....

You have 5 seconds to answer each question.

1. .... | 80 |

2. ....

3. ....

4. ....

5. .... | 30 |

You have 10 seconds to answer each question.

6. ....

Cost of 1 kg	
lemons	75p
limes	85p
grapes	£2.20

7. .... | 50 |

8. .... | 210 |

9. .... | 7.4, 7.7 |

79

Mental Arithmetic Test

10.

11. $\frac{1}{6}$ $\frac{1}{60}$ $\frac{6}{600}$ $\frac{6}{10}$ $\frac{6}{100}$

12 ....cm

13. .... | 74 |

14. .... | 374 |

15. .... | 90% |

You have 15 seconds to answer each question.

16. .... | 52, 55, 58 |

17. ....

18. | 25   50   45   100   250 |

19. ....

20. .... | £1.50 |

80